Vicariou
Lutheran Cate
an

T. R. Halvorson

Synoptic Text Information Services, Inc.
Sidney, Montana

Synoptic Text

Synoptic Text Information Services, Inc.
303 3rd Street SE, Sidney, MT 59270

Amazon KDP Paperback Edition
ISBN: 9798375670010
Imprint: Independently published

Contents

Preface

Lutheran Orthodoxy teaches that a vital part of the work of God in Christ is atonement by vicarious satisfaction. Vicarious satisfaction is attested in Scripture, the Lutheran confessions in the Book of Concord, explanations of the Catechism, Lutheran hymns, the liturgy, the Sacraments, and so on.

Nevertheless, the atonement is in controversy in Lutheran circles. The adversaries deny vicarious satisfaction. They substitute a general amnesty that is announced in a bloodless absolution. According to them, the cross would not have been necessary had sinners only believed that God can and does just "up and forgive." In their teaching, the cross does not win salvation. It is used to convince sinners of a sheer absolution that was available before and without the cross.

In a nutshell, the adversaries essentially deny Apology of the Augsburg Confession, Article V, paragraph 101:

> We are justified only when we receive Christ as the Atoning Sacrifice and believe that for Christ's sake God is reconciled to us. Neither is justification even to be dreamed of without Christ as the Atonement.

Chapter One provides a formulation of the orthodox doctrine of vicarious satisfaction, lists the witnesses to vicarious satisfaction, provides preliminary evidence that there is a current controversy about the atonement in our circles, states what the controversy is, outlines the teachings of the adversaries, shows that the controversy is an old one, and briefly sketches the rhetorical tactics of the adversaries.

Chapters Two through Four survey three of the witnesses to

vicarious satisfaction: explanations of Luther's Small Catechism, the Lutheran confessions in the Book of Concord, and Lutheran hymns.

Chapter One

Confession and Controversy

Formulation of Vicarious Satisfaction

Lutheran Orthodoxy teaches that an indispensable part of the mighty work that God has done in Christ is atonement by vicarious satisfaction. This is not the only aspect of the atonement. The atonement is a manifold panoply of salvation.[1] But vicarious satisfaction remains indispensable, and some of the other aspects are grounded upon vicarious satisfaction. They are effects of Christ making satisfaction for us.

From a survey of explanations of the *Small Catechism*, we may draw a useable formulation of vicarious satisfaction. Jesus made satisfaction to God for us under the Law in two ways.

- **Active Obedience.** On our behalf He lived a life of active obedience under the Law. He fulfilled all righteousness for us under the Law.

- **Passive Obedience.** On our behalf He rendered passive obedience to God. He did this by his innocent suffering of the Law's penalty of death.

Vicarious satisfaction presupposes the fall into sin; God's

---

[1] Scripture speaks of atonement in words and themes of covenant, testament, sacrifice, Day of Atonement, Passover, Pascal Lamb, redemption, reconciliation, propitiation, justification, the blood of Christ, Lamb of God, payment, Surety, covering, mercy-seat, deliverance, victory over our enemies (the Devil, the world, our sinful selves, death), and ransom, to name some. Themes of Christus Victor, ransom, and others hold prominent places in Lutheran theology along with vicarious satisfaction.

justice; the accusation, verdict, judgment, condemnation, and curse of God's Law; and God's truthfulness and trustworthiness in his Law. It confesses Christ as our substitute, who stood condemned in our place under God's justice and God's Law. It confesses that by imputation our sins were charged to Christ and by imputation his righteousness by both active and passive obedience is given to us.

> Jesus's suffering and death is called "vicarious" Atonement. A vicar is one who acts for someone else, in someone else's stead. Jesus suffered in our stead.[2]

"God sent forth His Son, born of a woman, born under the law, to redeem those who were under the law." (Galatians 4:4) "For He made Him who knew no sin to be sin for us, that we might become the righteousness of God in Him." (2 Corinthians 5:21) "How much more shall the blood of Christ, who through the eternal Spirit offered Himself without spot to God, cleanse your conscience from dead works to serve the living God?" (Hebrews 9:14)

God demonstrated his satisfaction with the redeeming work of Christ by resurrecting him from the dead (Romans 4:25). God announces his satisfaction by his "word of reconciliation" (2 Corinthians 5:19) which He proclaims by the apostles and pastors in the "ministry of reconciliation" (2 Corinthians 5:18).

God is "just and the justifier of the one who has faith in Jesus." (Romans 3:26). In that saying we see both Law and Gospel. We see both justice and mercy. We see Law in the word "just." We see Gospel in the words "justifier" and "faith." In the atonement, neither God's justice nor his Law is arbitrarily set aside. Instead, Christ fulfills and satisfies justice and the Law.

---

[2] J. A. Dell, *Senior Catechism: Luther's Small Catechism in Question and Answer Form* (Columbus, OH: The Wartburg Press, 1939), 103.

The adversaries[3] say vicarious satisfaction has no Gospel. They say it is not gracious, merciful, or loving because justice and the Law were satisfied. Their critique overlooks that it was not satisfied by us guilty sinners, but by our Mediator, Vicar, and Substitute. A stroke of justice pierced Christ, and by a gift of grace God imputes his death and righteousness to us. Both of God's Words, Law and Gospel, are trustworthy.

Recapping, the elements of vicarious satisfaction are:

- God's justice, Law, verdict, judgment, condemnation, and curse
- Substitution
- Active obedience
- Passive obedience
- Imputation, counting, reckoning
- Satisfaction

These elements are facets of the jewel of atonement for which we thank, praise, serve, and obey Christ. They also are an index of denials of atonement by the adversaries. This list of elements catalogs the angles of attack on vicarious satisfaction. In every attack, one or more of these elements are denied.

Orientation of Sin and Consequences, Atonement and Benefits

Vicarious satisfaction does not exclude *Christus Victor* (victory over and deliverance from our enemies) but explains it and gives it its ground. As Luther explains in the Large

---

[3] The meaning and scope of the term "the adversaries" as used here is given under the heading "What Is the Controversy?" It is being used as a designation of a school of theological thought. It is a composite of what multiple members of that school teach, but it must be remembered that no school is a monolith. Not everything that is said of the school as a whole is necessarily true of every member of the school.

Catechism, the devil is God's mask and jailer based on our guilt under the Law. Once Christ by vicarious satisfaction reverses God verdict of guilty to innocent, the devil and all other enemies lose their legal custody, and thereby we are delivered from our enemies.[4]

Theodore Dierks

Sin has manifold ill consequences. The work of Christ in atonement is a manifold panoply of salvation. Scripture speaks of atonement using a variety of words and themes.[5] It is important to understand, as Theodore Dierks lucidly explains,[6] that the orientation of sin and its consequences affects the orientation of atonement and its benefits.

While sinners suffer physical and spiritual death, bondage to sin, bondage to the devil, lostness, blindness, darkness, inherited corruption, and inability to deliver themselves from these conditions, Dierks says Christ and the Apostles orient these as the consequences of legal guilt. These consequences are judgments and punishments of God for the guilt of sin. Bondage to the devil is not of the devil's own power or right but exists by God using the devil as an executioner of judgment.

---

[4] Albrecht Peters, trans. Thomas H. Trapp, *Commentary on Luther's Catechisms, Creed* (Concordia Publishing House, St. Louis: 2011), 161-162; Jack D. Kilcrease, *The Doctrine of the Atonement from Luther to Forde* (Eugene, Oregon: Wipf & Stock, 2018), 28-29, 44, 48; and Theodore Dierks, *Reconciliation and Justification* (St Louis: Concordia Publishing House, 1938), 19, 43-44.

[5] Scripture speaks of atonement in words and themes of covenant, testament, sacrifice, Day of Atonement, Passover, Pascal Lamb, redemption, reconciliation, propitiation, justification, the blood of Christ, Lamb of God, payment, Surety, covering, mercy-seat, deliverance, victory over our enemies (the Devil, the world, our sinful selves, death), and ransom, to name some. In Scripture and in dogmatics, these words and themes have usually related and sometimes partially overlapping meanings. Yet each remains a distinct theme.

[6] Theodore Dierks, *Reconciliation and Justification*, (St Louis: Concordia Publishing House, 1938).

Why is man unable to free himself from the bondage of sin? It is because he cannot remove his guilt. As long as he is guilty, he is under the bondage of sin because of the judgment of God; and as long he is under bondage, he can only heap guilt upon guilt.[7]

"The devil is merely God's executioner, carrying out the judgments of God."[8] "If God no longer pronounces condemnation on the sinner, the devil can no longer rule over such a one."[9] "Since the guilt of sin has been made of none effect, man has also been redeemed from eternal death."[10] "Since the guilt of sin has been cancelled, man is also delivered from the power of the devil."[11] "Because the guilt of sin has been erased, therefore we are no longer under the judgment of God to suffer the penalty of guilt, i.e., to be under the bondage of sin, death, and the devil."[12] "In all this, the blotting out of the guilt of sin by the self-sacrifice of Christ must always be emphasized as the cause and source of redemption from sin, death, and the power of the devil."[13]

In order to efface the guilt of sin, God sent His only-begotten Son into the world to take the place of sinful man. Of Him God demanded perfect obedience to His holy Law, and imputing to Him the guilt of all sins of all men, He demanded that He pay the penalty. Through His vicarious satisfaction, or atonement, Christ turned the wrath of God into grace and favor. In other words, in Christ, God

---

[7] Dierks, *Reconciliation and Justification*, 19.

[8] Dierks, *Reconciliation and Justification*, 43.

[9] Dierks, *Reconciliation and Justification*, 43.

[10] Dierks, *Reconciliation and Justification*, 43.

[11] Dierks, *Reconciliation and Justification*, 43.

[12] Dierks, *Reconciliation and Justification*, 44.

[13] Dierks, *Reconciliation and Justification*, 43.

reconciled the world unto Himself, not imputing their trespasses unto them (objective justification); and whoever believes and accepts this reconciliation has forgiveness and pardon (subjective justification).[14]

Albrecht Peters

As Albrecht Peters explains in his consummate five-volume commentary on Luther's catechisms, this orientation accords with Luther's teaching in the *Large Catechism*.

> The reformer thus takes up both constellations of motifs: on the one hand, Christ as the one who vanquishes all the powers of destruction and powers of death and, on the other hand, Christ as our substitute and as our propitiatory offering over against God's holy, judging wrath. Luther links both aspects in such a way that the hidden emphasis from the Western Church and the Middle Ages, on the punishing suffering of Christ, persists. The propitiation of God's wrath remains the center, in terms of content, in the catechisms as well; at the deepest level, it is God's curse of judgment that delivers us over to the powers of destruction. These powers stand in a unique relationship with God; according to the Large Catechism, on the one hand, they are our "tyrants," caught up in rebellion against God, and yet, on the other hand, they are the "harsh schoolmasters" that God Himself put in place, which means that they are the authorities who run the prison; the real prison came into existence for us when God gave us over under the condemning wrath of His Law. "Death, sin, hell, all of these come from the wrath of God; they are its harsh schoolmasters." Even among these ominous allies,

---

[14] Dierks, *Reconciliation and Justification*, 21.

Luther intimates that there is a pecking order; Satan stands at the top; he "clearly is to be identified as a prince over sin and the prince of death." This is the specifically theological dimension; to it corresponds an anthropological aspect. As we are free, in heart and conscience, from the accusation of the Law and from the wrath of God that thereby brings its onslaught, we are free, as well, with respect to the battle against the satanic demons; for us, these have been rendered harmless, because the wrath of God no longer stands behind them.

By means of these insights, Luther deepens and personifies both the "classical theory of the atonement" of the Christus Victor model as well as Anselm's teaching about satisfaction. By means of his hyper-realistic and drastic images of Christ's victory over the dark comrades, sin, death and the devil, he reaches back into the tradition of the early Church and the Eastern Church and renews its emphasis on the motif of a battle that encompasses the entire earth. But because he points out, in, with and under the onslaughts of the powers of death, how Christ fully suffers the deepest, holy wrath of judgment from God that hangs over all human guilt, and inserts the Law at this point as well, into the list of the powers that effect the curse, the reformer deepens the early Church's confession about Christus Victor by means of insights that are set forth initially by Paul: precisely by suffering the full consequences of the divine curse of judgment upon the guilt of human sin, Jesus Christ overcomes the original power of those that destroy.[15]

---

[15] Albrecht Peters, trans. Thomas H. Trapp, *Commentary on Luther's Catechisms, Creed* 2 (Concordia Publishing House, St. Louis: 2011), 161-162.

Francis Pieper

Francis Pieper teaches this orientation.

> Since Christ reconciled mankind with God, that is canceled their guilt, makind is delivered from all the terrible consequences of guilt, from death, from the power of the devil, from the dominion of sin, etc. Scripture describes at great length this effect of reconciliation. ... But all of this, our deliverance from all evil, is due to our deliverance from sin. Scripture constantly reminds us that our deliverance from the guilt of sin through the one sacrifice of Christ must be kept in the foreground. Because our guilt is wiped out before God, therefore we are also redeemed from death, etc.[16]

Jack D. Kilcrease

In his critique of Anselm, Aulén failed to recognize Luther's harmonization in the Large Catechism as just explained from Peters' commentary, which accords with Dierks' orientation stated above. Aulén did not recognize *Christus Victor* in coordination with or complementary to Anselm. Rather, "Anselm is judged not simply inadequate, but anathema."[17]

Jack D. Kilcrease also takes up the questions: How did the tyrants get their power over us? How did our enemies get their grip? They got it because of the just verdict of the Law that we are sinners. Kilcrease summarizes this piece of Theodosius Harnack's presentation of Luther's view:

> The law was an eternal and objective standard that needed to be fulfilled by sinful humanity. The

---

[16] Francis Pieper, *Christian Dogmatics*, vol. II (St. Louis: Concordia Publishing House, 1951), II.343-344.

[17] Peter J. Scaer, "The Atonement in Mark's Sacramental Theology." *Concordia Theological Quarterly*, vol. 72, no. 3, 2008, pp. 227-242, 227.

demonic forces that held humanity in their sway (law, death, and the devil) were not masters who had assumed their offices arbitrarily. Rather, these forces dominated the world because of human sin, and were manifestations of God's wrath.[18]

Kilcrease summarizes this piece of Luther's view directly from Luther in the Large Catechism:

> Luther's combination of the two motifs becomes even more pronounced and explicit in his more-detailed account of the Large Catechism. First, the Large Catechism clarifies how bondage to the devil and the wrath and law of God are connected.
>
> "For when we had been created by God the Father, and had received from Him all manner of good, the devil came and led us into disobedience, sin, death, and all evil, so that we fell under His [God's] wrath and displeasure and were doomed to eternal damnation, as we had merited and deserved."
>
> In other words, the demonic forces of the world gained their power over human beings as a result of sin. The devil led human beings into sin, thereby making them slaves to "sin, death and all evil." The violation of God's law incurred his wrath, which allowed humans to be held by these powers of darkness. These forces serve as a mask of God's infinite wrath against sin.[19]

On the basis of this judgment of the Law, we are given over to jailors, who are our enemies, the tyrants that hold us: the devil, the world, the sinful self, and the Law (because by the

---

[18] Jack D. Kilcrease, *The Doctrine of the Atonement from Luther to Forde* (Eugene, OR: Wipf & Stock, 2018), 28-29.

[19] Kilcrease, *The Doctrine of the Atonement from Luther to Forde*, 44.

flesh it is weak, Romans 8:3). That being so, through the cross, Jesus achieves not just one but both of our needs. God accepts the active obedience of Christ for us and his innocent suffering of the penalty of the Law for us. This vicarious satisfaction reverses the verdict of Law that was against us. Since the judgment of the Law was the basis of the grip of our enemies, the reversal of the verdict also looses their grip upon us. They no longer have the legal authority that our prior verdict of guilt gave them. Thus they are conquered and we are delivered. Their former lawful custody now is unlawful thanks to Christ.

In the cross, Christ accomplished both parts of a unified atonement for us. He is at once our penal substitute and our conquering deliverer.

This is the beautiful harmonization of two views of the atonement, vicarious satisfaction and the conquest of our enemies. Adding to the beauty is how the harmonization prioritizes justification. Christ openly triumphs over the tyrants of darkness in the cross, but He does so by breaking their legal authority under the former verdict of guilt that now is washed away by his blood.

By rendering infinite satisfaction and neutralizing the threat of the law, Christ is also victorious over the demonic forces of the old creation. All these forces are masks of God's wrath, in that "the whole creation is a face or mask of God." The powers of darkness enslave and define persons living apart from the grace of God. When the law is satisfied, the proclamation of the word of God first kills and then breathes new life into the person of faith:

"I am crucified with Christ." Paul adds this word because he wants to explain how the Law is devoured by the Law. . . When by this faith I am crucified and die to the Law, then the Law loses all its jurisdiction over me, as it lost it over Christ. Thus, just as Christ Himself was crucified to the

> Law, sin, death, and the Devil, so that they have no further jurisdiction over Him, so through faith I, having been crucified with Christ in spirit, am crucified and die to the Law, sin, etc., so that they have no further jurisdiction over me but are now crucified and dead to me."[20]

I read the first three chapters of Kilcrease's *The Doctrine of the Atonement from Luther to Forde* in an airplane on the way to an LCMS synodical convention and re-experienced the epiphany as when I had read Peters' commentary on the Large Catechism. Then at the convention, Rev. William Weedon, Convention Chaplain, had selected a reading from Zephaniah for one of the services of daily worship. Get a load of this:

> "The Lord has taken away the judgments against you; he has cleared away your enemies." (Zephaniah 3:15)

Wham! There both achievements of the cross are together in a half verse. "The Lord has taken away the judgments against you." Vicarious satisfaction. "He has cleared away your enemies." Conquest of our enemies. The judgments are removed first, and that also clears away our enemies.

So, in Lutheran theology, we do affirm, and prominently so, the victory of Christ over his and our enemies. We affirm our deliverance from their tyranny. The atonement would be incomplete without this. But the basis of the defeat of our enemies is the removal of the legal guilt that was the basis for their executioner status. Thus, vicarious satisfaction must remain in the proclamation of the Gospel, and its orientation as the basis of the manifold benefits of the atonement must remain.

---

[20] Kilcrease, *The Doctrine of the Atonement from Luther to Forde*, 48, quoting Luther and citing LW 26:165; WA 40.I:280.

Witnesses To Vicarious Satisfaction

Host of Witnesses

Vicarious satisfaction as taught in Lutheran Orthodoxy has the support of

- Scripture
- Luther
- The confessions in the Book of Concord (see Chapter Three)
- Explanations of the Catechism (see Chapter Two)
- Lutheran hymns (see Chapter Four)
- Lutheran liturgy
- Baptism
- The Lord's Supper
- Lutheran dogmatics
- The Brief Statement of the Missouri Synod.
- A host of modern confessors including Theodore Dierks, Junius Remensnyder, Francis Pieper, Jack D. Kilcrease, David Scaer, Peter Scaer, John Kleinig, Robert Preus, Kurt Marquart, Charles Gieschern, Burnell Eckardt, Jr., Andrew Preus, Jeffrey Gibbs, Arthur Just, and Walter Maier

This is a huge field that, when retraced, touches on nearly everything in the Christian religion.

Scripture

The witness of Scripture to Christ's vicarious satisfaction is so replete that it is not possible to set if forth here beyond the passages here quoted. Additional passages teaching vicarious satisfaction are quoted or referenced in the Book of Concord, explanations of the Catechism, and in our dogmatics texts such as Pieper, Melanchthon, Chemnitz, and Gerhard. In some of those you will find atonement under the topic of justification and in others under Christ's office of Mediator.

The treatment by Johannes Andreas Quenstedt in his *Theologia Didactico-polemica sive systema theolgicum* (1685), Part Three, Cap. III, Membrum II, "De officio Christi," Sec. 1, Th. 14 to 44., belongs here. Robert D. Preus says of it:

> The strong exegetical basis for his entire treatment will be noticeable throughout. Quenstedt's systematic section on the Atonement actually presents nothing but exegesis of passages pertaining to the doctrine, arranged according to a quite skeletal scholastic outline. The reader will notice, too, how very closely Quenstedt's terminology and understanding of this great doctrine approximate what has always been believed and taught concerning the vicarious atonement within conservative Lutheranism.[21]

Therefore, for a presentation of the witness of Scripture to vicarious satisfaction, I can refer you to the new publication *Atonement in Lutheran Orthodoxy: Johannes Quenstedt*,[22] containing the first translation into English of Quenstedt's "De officio Christi," Sec. 1, Th. 14 to 44.

Luther

As with Scripture, time and space here would not allow even a representative sampling of Luther's expressions of vicarious satisfaction because there are so many.

The adversaries like to use Luther's *frohlicher wechsel*, "the joyous exchange," or "the wonderful exchange" as if it were

---

[21] Robert D. Preus, "The Vicarious Atonement in John Quenstedt," Concordia Theological Monthly, vol. xxxii, no. 2, 1961, pp. 78-97, 79.

[22] Johannes Quenstedt and Robert D. Preus, *Atonement in Lutheran Orthodoxy: Johannes Quenstedt*, Matthew Carver, trans. (Sidney, Montana: Synoptic Text Information Services, Inc. 2023).

evidence against vicarious satisfaction. Therefore, let it suffice for present purposes to see that they have distorted what Luther said, and then used the distortion as their evidence. Let us look at his raw words themselves, and each of you decide whether these words deny or confess vicarious satisfaction. In a commentary on Psalm 22 in 1519, which Luther regarded as "a prophesy of the suffering and resurrection of Christ and a prophecy of the Gospel,"[23] Luther says:

> [5] Atque hoc est mysterium illud opulentum gratiae divinae in peccatores, quod admirabili commertio peccata nostra iam non nostra, sed Christi sunt, et iustitia Christi non Christi, sed nostra est. Exinanivit enim se illa, ut nos ea indueret et impleret, et replevit se nostris, ut exinaniret nos eisdem, ita ut iam non modo obiective (ut dicunt) sit nostra Christi iustitia, sed et [10] formaliter, sicut non tantum obiective Christi sunt peccata nostra, sed et formaliter. Quo modo enim ille in nostris peccatis dolet et confunditur, hoc modo nos in illius iustitia laetamur et gloriamur, at ipse revera et formaliter in illis dolet, ut hic videmus.[24]

which may be rendered,

> [5] And this is that rich mystery of divine grace for sinners, that by a wonderful exchange our sins are no longer ours, but Christ's and the righteousness of Christ is not Christ's but ours, for He emptied himself of his righteousness that He might clothe us with it and fill us with it, and He filled himself with our sin, that he might empty us

---

[23] Martin Luther, *Reading the Psalms with Luther* (St. Louis: Concordia Publishing House, 2007), 56.

[24] *D. Martin Luthers Werke*, Kritische Gesamtausgabe (Critical Complete Edition), (Weimar: Herman Böhlau, 1892), 5:608.5-10 (*Operationes in Psalmos*, 1519-1521).

to the same, so that Christ's righteousness is no longer just objectively (as they say) ours, but also [10] formally, just as our sins are not only objectively Christ's, but also formally. For in the same way that he suffers and is confounded in our sins, in this way we rejoice and glory in his righteousness, but he really and formally suffers in them, as we see here.

We saw already under the headings of Albrecht Peters and Jack D. Kilcrease in the section "Orientation of Sin and Consequences; Atonement and Benefits" how Luther harmonized vicarious satisfaction with *Christus Victor* in the Large Catechism. We may see Luther's confession of vicarious satisfaction also in SA II.i.1–5, SA III.iii.38, LC II.31, and LC IV.37. In LC II.31 he says, "He suffered, died, and was buried so that He might make satisfaction for me and pay what I owe, not with silver or gold, but with His own precious blood. In SA III.iii.38 he says,

> [38] Neither can the satisfaction be uncertain, because it is not our uncertain, sinful work. Rather, it is the suffering and blood of the innocent Lamb of God, who takes away the sin of the world [John 1:29].

In *The Doctrine of the Atonement from Luther to Forde*, Kilcrease does the heavy lifting of examining the evidence upon which Forde bases his errors. In some cases, Forde cites passages from Luther that refute Forde and maintain the orthodox Lutheran view. In other cases, as wild as this might seem, Forde actually has no basis at all. He merely asserts premises that his argument needs simply because his argument needs them. I can't bet the farm on that, and neither should you.

Brief Statement LCMS 1932

The "Brief Statement of the Doctrinal Position of The Lutheran Church—Missouri Synod (1932)," says:

> The purpose of this miraculous incarnation of the

Son of God was that He might become the Mediator between God and men, both fulfilling the divine Law and suffering and dying in the place of mankind. In this manner God reconciled the whole sinful world unto Himself, Gal. 4:4, 5; 3:13; 2 Cor. 5:18, 19." (Article 8, "Of Redemption.")

In that statement we see substitution in the words "in the place of mankind." We see active obedience in the words "fulfilling the divine Law." We see passive obedience in "suffering and dying." We see satisfaction in the words, "In this manner God reconciled the whole sinful world unto Himself." We see God's justice, Law, verdict, judgment, condemnation, and curse in the assertion that the suffering and dying was "in the place of mankind."

We also see nearly all the elements of vicarious satisfaction referenced in the title "Mediator between God and men." The office of Christ as mediator has two parts: his sacrifice of himself in our place to make satisfaction for us; and his intercession with the Father on our behalf.

This part of His work is called the *Sacerdotal Office*. "The sacerdotal office consists in this, that Christ holds a middle ground between God and men, who are at variance with each other, so that He offers sacrifice and prayers that He may reconcile man with God." (Br., 491) Accordingly it is subdivided into two parts, corresponding to the two functions that belong to priests, i. e., the offering of sacrifice and intercessory prayer. ... The first part is called *satisfaction*, by which expression, at the same time, the reason is implied why reconciliation with God was possible only through a sacrifice; because thereby satisfaction was to be rendered to God, who had been offended by our sins, and therefor demanded punishment.[25]

Preliminary Evidence of Controversy

Many notable Lutheran voices have raised concerns about the teaching of Christ's work of atonement "in our circles"[26] and "in our church."[27] These voices include:

- Presenters at a four-day symposium at Concordia Theological Seminary in Fort Wayne in 2008.

- Authors of follow-up articles published in the *Concordia Theological Quarterly*.[28]

- Presenters at a congress on the Lutheran confessions organized by the Association of Confessional Lutherans and the Luther Academy in 2019.[29]

- Presenters at another symposium at the seminary in Fort Wayne in 2020 organized because, since their 2008 symposium, matters had gotten worse.[30]

- The considerable work of Jack D. Kilcrease in his 2009 doctoral dissertation, *The Self-Donation of God: Gerhard Forde and the Question of Atonement in the Lutheran*

---

[25] Heinrich Schmid, *The Doctrinal Theology of the Evangelical Lutheran Church*, 3rd ed., rev. Charles A. Hay and Henry E. Jacobs (Minneapolis: Augsburg Publishing House, 1899), 342-43.

[26] Charles A. Gieschen, "Editorial." *Concordia Theological Quarterly*, vol. 72, no. 3, 2008, p. 194.

[27] Arthur A. Just, Jr., "The Cross, the Atonement, and the Eucharist in Luke." *Concordia Theological Quarterly*, vol. 84, no. 3-4, 2020, pp. 227-244, 228.

[28] Volume 72, no. 4 (2008).

[29] The Association of Confessional Lutherans' National Free Conference No. 30 and the Luther Academy's Lecture Series No. 26, "A Congress on the Lutheran Confessions" on the theme "Antinomianism Old & New: The Return of Seminex Theology in Light of the Lutheran Confessions."

[30] Presenters and paper authors for the 2008 and 2020 seminary symposia included Charles P. Arand, Simon J. Gathercole, Charles A. Gieschen, Jeffrey A. Gibbs, Arthur A. Just Jr., John W. Kleinig, Timo Laato, Noamichi Masaki, John A. Maxfield, Walter A. Maier III, Jeffrey H. Pulse, Lawrence R. Rast, Jr., Michael J. Root, David P. Scaer, Peter J. Scaer, and William C. Weinrich.

Tradition,[31] subsequently developed into a book in 2013;[32] his lecture at a symposium at Fort Wayne in 2011 published the next year in *Concordia Theological Quarterly* as "Atonement and Justification in Gerhard Forde: A Confessional Lutheran Response;"[33] his 2018 book, *The Doctrine of the Atonement from Luther to Forde*;[34] and his 2018 journal article, "Johann Gerhard, the Socinians, and Modern Rejections of Substitutionary Atonement."[35]

At the 2020 Fort Wayne symposium, Arthur A. Just, Jr. exclaimed:

> It seems incredible that there are theological forces in our church that prompted an exegetical symposium at Fort Wayne in 2020 addressing *The Cross, the Atonement, and the Wrath of God*. As Lutherans, how could these things not be unquestioned among us as central to the heart of our theology, the essence of biblical theology? How can Lutherans tell the story of the Bible apart from the cross and the atonement?[36]

---

[31] Jack D. Kilcrease, *The Self-Donation of God: Gerhard Forde and the Question of Atonement in the Lutheran Tradition, Dissertation*, Marquette University (2009).

[32] Jack D. Kilcrease, *The Self-Donation of God: A Contemporary Lutheran approach to Christ and His Benefits* (Eugene, OR: Wipf & Stock, 2013).

[33] Jack D. Kilcrease, "Atonement and Justification in Gerhard Forde: A Confessional Lutheran Response," *Concordia Theological Quarterly*, vol 76, nos. 3-42, 2012, pp. 269-293.

[34] Jack D. Kilcrease, *The Doctrine of the Atonement from Luther to Forde* (Eugene, OR: Wipf & Stock, 2018).

[35] Jack D. Kilcrease, "Johann Gerhard, the Socinians, and Modern Rejections of Substitutionary Atonement." *Concordia Theological Quarterly* 82, no. 1-2 (2018), 19-44.

[36] Just, *op cit.*, 228. He then provided a thorough debunking of a theological myth that Luke has no doctrine of atonement. Luke has a doctrine of sacrificial vicarious atonement with an accent on its liturgical delivery in pastoral ministry in the Lord's Supper.

Another 2020 symposium presenter, John W. Kleinig, said,

> confessional Lutheran teaching has recently been challenged on many fronts by those who cannot stomach this whole "bloody" business. In our own circles, the most forceful attack on this teaching has come from those who are uneasy about the propitiation of God's wrath by Christ's sacrificial death. They separate justification from its foundation in Christ's atoning death and his fulfilment of God's law by what he suffered on our behalf.[37]

What Is the Controversy

Across Christendom today, there are many forms of denial of vicarious satisfaction. Our focus here is limited to denials that have the most significant circulation in our circles and church. In this limited sense we will use the designation "the adversaries."[38] Roughly speaking, the adversaries are Gerhard O. Forde and his disciples. Tributaries to this stream include the Socinians, Gustaf Aulén, and Johannes Von Hofmann.

The Adversaries' Method

The adversaries:

- describe Anselm's penal substitution,
- treat that as if it were the whole position of Lutheran Orthodoxy,[39]

---

[37] John W. Kleinig, "Sacrificial Atonement by Jesus and God's Wrath in the Light of the Old Testament," *Concordia Theological Quarterly*, vol. 84, no. 3-4, 2020, pp. 195-208, 195.

[38] As stated in n. 3 p. 3, the term "the adversaries" is being used as a designation of a school of theological thought. It is a composite of what multiple members of that school teach, but it must be remembered that no school is a monolith. Not everything that is said of the school as a whole is necessarily true of every member of the school.

[39] Forde may be credited with recognizing Lutheran "orthodoxy differs from

- subject that caricature of Lutheran Orthodoxy to a critique,

- use earlier critiques by Peter Abelard, the Socinians, and Gustaf Aulén,

- use the development of those critiques by Johannes Von Hofmann,[40]

- use a Neo-Orthodox approach to Scripture and doctrine,

- reject Lutheran Orthodoxy on the atonement, and

- substitute for vicarious satisfaction a sheer and bloodless word of so-called absolution, what Forde calls "up and forgive"

"Up and Forgive"

Forde developed his atonement doctrine in many of his writings. [41] An oft-cited example is his 1983 essay "Caught in the Act: Reflections on the Work of Christ."[42] There he rejected the orthodox Lutheran doctrine. He replaced

---

Anselm in its emphasis upon active obedience in the fulfillment of the law as well as passive obedience." [39] Gerhard O. Forde, "The Position of Orthodoxy," in Gerhard O. Forde, *The Essential Forde: Distinguishing Law and Gospel*, eds. Nicholas Hopman, Mark C. Mattes, and Steven D. Paulson (Minneapolis: Fortress Press, 2019), 39. Nevertheless, the school on the whole acts as though when they refute defects in Anselm they have refuted Lutheran Orthodoxy.

[40] Jack D. Kilcrease, "*Heilsgeschicte* and Atonement in the Theology of Johannes Christian Konrad von Hofmann (1810-1877): An Exposition and Critique," *Logia: A Journal of Lutheran Theology* 22, no. 2 (2013).

[41] For an exposition of Forde's doctrine drawn from his dogmatics text (Gerhard Forde, "The Work of Christ," in *Christian Dogmatics* 2 vols., ed. Carl E. Braaten and Robert W. Jenson (Philadelphia: Fortress, 1984), 2:3–99.) and one of his books (Gerhard Forde, *Where God Meets Man: Luther's Down-to-Earth Approach to the Gospel* (Minneapolis: Augsburg, 1972)), see Walter A. Maier III, "Penal Substitutionary Atonement?" *Concordia Theological Quarterly*, vol. 84, no. 3-4, 2020, pp. 245-263.

[42] Gerhard O. Forde, "Caught in the Act: Reflections on the Work of Christ," *World in World*, 3/1 1983, pp. 22-31.

vicarious satisfaction with, to use his own phrase, an "up and forgive" theory. Before and without the sacrifice of Christ, God just up and forgave sin, he says.

Three times in "Caught in the Act" Forde poses the question, why could not God just up and forgive without the cross and, for that matter, without the incarnation.

> The persistent criticism of doctrines of vicarious satisfaction and substitutionary atonement since the enlightenment have the same root. The picture painted of God is too black, too contrary to the biblical witness. If the death was payment, how could reconciliation be an act of mercy? Mercy is mercy, not the result of payment. If God is by nature love and mercy, why could he not just up and forgive? Jesus, it seems, forgave sins *before* his death. Why then was the death necessary?[43]

> So we come back to our original question: Why the murder of the innocent one? What does that accomplish for us—or for God? What is "the word" of Christ? What does he actually do for us that God could not have done with greater ease and economy in some other way? The crucial and persistent question emerging from discussion of the various views seems always to be that of the necessity for the concrete and actual work of Christ among us. It is, of course, ultimately the question of the necessity for Christology at all. Cannot God just up and forgive and/or cast out demons? Or to use another current form of the question: Is there not grace aplenty in the Old Testament? Or in nature? Or in other religions even? Why Jesus? Why the New

---

[43] Forde, "Caught in the Act," 23.

Testament?[44]

> Why could not God just up and forgive? Let us start there. If we look at the narrative about Jesus, the actual events themselves, the "brute facts" as they have come down to us, the answer is quite simple. He did! Jesus came preaching repentance and forgiveness, declaring the bounty and mercy of his "Father." The problem, however, is that we could not buy that. And so we killed him. And just so we are caught in the act.[45]

In the "up and forgive" theory, atonement happens not on the cross but when a sheer, bloodless word of absolution is believed.

Forde died in 2005, but as Forde disciple Steven D. Paulson[46] says in the title to his 2019 essay in *The Essential Forde: Distinguishing Law and Gospel*, "Forde Lives!"[47] He lives in the ongoing work of "his disciples Timothy Wengert, James Nestingen, Steven Paulson, and, more recently, Nicholas Hopman,"[48] among others.

Paulson and Mark C. Mattes in their 2017 "Introduction" to an anthology of Forde's writings, *A More Radical Gospel: Essays on Eschatology, Authority, Atonement, and Ecumenism*, track Forde saying:

> Indeed, why is Christ's death *necessary* at all? Forde's radical response is that—it was not! Why could God

---

[44] Forde, "Caught in the Act," 25.

[45] Forde, "Caught in the Act," 26.

[46] David P. Scaer, "Is Law Intrinsic to God's Essence," *Concordia Theological Quarterly*, vol. 82, nos. 1-2, 2020, 5.

[47] Steven D. Paulson, "Forde Lives!" in Gerhard O. Forde, *The Essential Forde: Distinguishing Law and Gospel*, eds. Nicholas Hopman, Mark C. Mattes, and Steven D. Paulson (Minneapolis: Fortress Press, 2019), 18-33.

[48] David P. Scaer, *op cit.*

not just forgive us? He did![49]

Paulson says again in "Forde Lives!", "The stupefied atonement question—Why could God not just up and forgive?—is answered simply: He did!"[50]

Sheer Absolution

Following Forde's lead about atonement happening not on the cross but only when a sheer word of absolution is believed, James Arne Nestingen teaches that,

> "[Christ] enters the conscience through the absolution, through the proclaimed Word and the administered Sacrament to effect the forgiveness of sin. This is the true substitutionary atonement, happening here and now."[51]

That removes atonement from the cross and installs it in our consciences. The adversaries speak of this kind of absolution as the proclamation of "the promise" of the Gospel. But according to the Apology of the Augsburg Confession, that is a half-gospel.

> [19] The second requirement for an atonement maker is that his merits are shown to make

---

[49] Mark C. Mattes and Steven D. Paulson, "Introduction" in Gerhard O. Forde, *A More Radical Gospel: Essays on Eschatology, Authority, Atonement, and Ecumenism* (Minneapolis: Fortress Press, 2017), xxv.

[50] Paulson, "Forde Lives!" 29.

[51] James Arne Nestingen, "Speaking of the End of the Law" in Albert B. Collver, Jr., James Arne Nestingen, and John T. Pless, eds., *The Necessary Distinction: A Continuing Conversation on Law & Gospel* (St. Louis: Concordia Publishing House, 20170, 174. In that passage, Nestingen says, "Christ finishes [note, not fulfills] the Law in two says." The first way is as quoted in the body here. The second way Jason D. Lane explains as "walking in the Law ... yet without compulsion (FC VI:18) "after justification." Jason D. Lane, "That I May Be His Own: The Necessary End of the Law," in Steven D. Paulson and Scott L. Keith, eds., *Handing Over the Goods* (Irvine, CA: 2018), 61. Hence, unless that walk is reclassified as being part of the atonement itself, that second way in Nestingen is not about the atonement itself but about one of its effects in the Christian life.

satisfaction for other people. They are divinely given to others, so that through them, just as by their own merits, other people may be regarded righteous. ...

[20] From both of these—the promise and the giving of merits—arises confidence in mercy. Such confidence in the divine promise, and likewise in Christ's merits, should be promoted when we pray. For we should be truly confident, both that for Christ's sake we are heard and that by His merits we have a reconciled Father.[52]

Their absolution "promises" but it does not give Christ's merits. It does not impute the obedience of Christ under the Law to us. The Apology says that from the two together, the promise and the giving of merits, confidence in mercy arises. In other words, faith grasps both the promise and the merits. A meritless promise is not the ground of what Scripture and the confessions call faith.

The Epitome of the Formula of Concord confesses "In His obedience alone, which as God and man He offered to the Father even to His death, He merited for us the forgiveness of sins and eternal life."[53] The Solid Declaration specifies the obedience of Christ as elemental to true absolution.

Christ's obedience alone—out of pure grace—is credited for righteousness through faith alone to all true believers. They are absolved from all their unrighteousness by this obedience.[54]

Catch that: absolved by Christ's obedience. Without vicarious satisfaction, there is no absolution. Sheer absolution is not Christian absolution. Again, the Solid Declaration confesses:

---

[52] Ap XXI.20

[53] Ep III.3.

[54] SD III.4.

A poor sinful person is justified before God, that is, absolved and declared free and exempt from all his sins and from the sentence of well-deserved condemnation, and is adopted into sonship and inheritance of eternal life, without any merit or worth of his own. This happens without any preceding, present, or subsequent works, out of pure grace, because of the sole merit, complete obedience, bitter suffering, death, and resurrection of our Lord Christ alone. His obedience is credited to us for righteousness.[55]

Yet again the Solid Declaration says,

Therefore, the righteousness that is credited to faith or to the believer out of pure grace is Christ's obedience, suffering, and resurrection, since He has made satisfaction for us to the Law and paid for <expiated> our sins. ... His obedience (not only in His suffering and dying, but also because He was voluntarily made under the Law in our place and fulfilled the Law by this obedience) is credited to us for righteousness. So, because of this complete obedience, which He rendered to His heavenly Father for us by doing and suffering and in living and dying, God forgives our sins. [56]

The promise, that is the Word of the Gospel, is the means of delivering the merits of Christ to us. "These treasures are brought to us by the Holy Spirit in the promise of the Holy Gospel."[57] "This righteousness is brought to us by the Holy Spirit through the Gospel and in the Sacraments. It is applied, taken, and received through faith."[58] Both are

---

[55] SD III.9.

[56] SD III.14–15.

[57] SD III.10.

[58] SD III.16.

necessary: the merits of Christ in vicarious satisfaction; and the delivery of them in the means of grace, the promise, the Gospel. The adversaries have an empty promise. They promise forgiveness apart from Christ's vicarious satisfaction. That is broth where chowder or stew should be.

The Solid Declaration says, "We trust that for the sake of His obedience alone we have the forgiveness of sins by grace, are regarded as godly and righteous by God the Father, and are eternally saved."[59]

Equivocation and Obfuscation

Nestingen's statement about "the true substitutionary atonement, happening here and now" in absolution appears in a publication from Concordia Publishing House, a synod-wide corporate entity of the Lutheran Church – Missouri Synod.[60] That qualifies as "in our circles" and "in our church." It is Synod's product that Synod directed CPH to publish for Synod by virtue of its prerogative to so direct under the bylaws of Synod. Thus, it is not a symptom of a rogue publishing house because CPH did not produce it but, as required, submitted to Synod's direction to publish Synod's product. As such, it is a symptom of Synod itself, not of CPH.

That book, *The Necessary Distinction: A Continuing Conversation on Law and Gospel*, is supposed to be about the distinction between Law and Gospel. But the parties do not use the terms "Law" and "Gospel" to mean the same things. Thus, there might be more talking past one another than continuing conversation. Though the heirs of Hofmann use traditional Lutheranesque language, the treatment suffers from equivocation. Kilcrease explains:

> As someone who regarded himself as Lutheran,

---

[59] SD III.11.

[60] *Bylaws of the Lutheran Church—Missouri Synod*, 1.2.1(w)(2); and 3.6.1(2).

Hofmann insisted that the structure of this historical revelation takes the shape of law and gospel. Nevertheless, law and gospel possess different meanings for Hofmann than they do in orthodox Lutheranism. Unlike in the Formula of Concord, Hofmann did not identify the law with the eternal and immutable commandments of God (*lex aeterna*) and various ways that those commandments relate to human existence under sin and grace (*triplex usus legis*). Instead, the law is to be seen primarily as the time of the old covenant, wherein there was a reign of divine wrath and mechanical legalism.[61]

Note the key element about time, "the time of the old covenant." Christ is the end of the Law not by fulfilling it for us but simply by changing one age to another, thus terminating the Law without vicarious satisfaction. Mark C. Mattes says,

> von Hofmann saw law ... as an epoch within the history of salvation. Likewise, Christ's atonement was no compensatory reckoning—that is, Christ dying in the place of sinners, an execution of a substitute. ... Forde proposes that law and gospel refer to two different ages: one (law) is past, and the other (gospel) is promised.[62]

Note again the element about time, "an epoch within the history of salvation." As David P. Scaer analyzes this, it is a type of dispensationalism, rather than proper distinction of Law and Gospel.

> Inherent in Hofmann's redefinition of atonement is a particular form of dispensationalism—the belief, still popular among some Evangelicals, that God

---

[61] Kilcrease, "Modern Rejections," 38.

[62] Mark C. Mattes, "Forde's Works: A Guide to The Essential Forde," in *The Essential Forde*, 9-10.

works differently in different periods of time (called "dispensations"). For Hofmann, law has a function only until the gospel comes.[63]

Forde himself speaks in similar language:

> The critical problem is the manner in which one conceives of the place of law in the theological system. Is the law as the orthodox system implied ... or is it, as Hofmann has said, only a part of a historical dispensation?[64]

Instead of having seven dispensations as in J. N. Darby (1800–1882), C. I. Scofield (1843–1921), and the *Scofield Reference Bible*, von Hofmann's *Heilsgeschichte* is a Lutheran two-dispensation Law-Gospel dispensationalism. Far from a toss-off characterization, Forde develops a chapter-length exposition of it in "Hoffman's *Heilsgeschichtliche* Scheme."[65] This is essentially an exogenous injection into Lutheran theology of German Idealism's view of history.[66] By it, "law is simply replaced by a historical scheme."[67]

As a concomitant of equivocation on the meanings of "Law" and "Gospel" is equivocation about what substitution means. Forde recasts the meaning of "in our place." Instead of referring to our standing before God's justice with an exchange of our sins and Christ's righteousness, the phrase means the occupation of our space, as can be pictured in the occupation of a city. Through this, he says, Jesus "atoned" by

---

[63] Scaer, "Is Law Intrinsic," 9.

[64] Gerhard O. Forde, "The Critical Problem: The Place of the Law in the Theological System," in *The Essential Ford*, 45.

[65] Gerhard O. Forde, *The Law-Gospel Debate* (Minneapolis: Augsburg Publishing House, 1969, 12-35.

[66] Forde, "The Critical Problem," 49.

[67] *Ibid.* To be fair to Forde himself, he issues a serious critique of von Hofmann's historical scheme, but his disciples do not seem to have appreciated the weight of that critique.

exchanging places without what Lutheran Orthodoxy means in vicarious satisfaction. In the process of speaking of this exchange, he sapped Luther's meaning of *frohlicher wechsel*, "the joyous exchange," or "the wonderful exchange"[68] as we saw earlier in Luther's commentary on Psalm 22. For Luther, the exchange is about our sins and Christ's righteousness. Forde rids substitution of the element of justice that Christians continue to sing:

> Many hands were raised to wound Him
> None would interpose to save
> But the deepest stroke that pierced Him
> Was the stroke that Justice gave[69]

Consistent with those changes, the meaning of "for Christ's sake" is changed. In Lutheran Orthodoxy, it means, as we pray in the Divine Service, "for the sake of his holy, innocent, and bitter sufferings and death of Your beloved Son, Jesus Christ, be gracious and merciful to me, a poor, sinful being."[70] In the Wisconsin Evangelical Lutheran Synod, pastors announce this Absolution: "By the perfect life and innocent death of our Lord Jesus Christ, he has removed your guilt forever."[71] In that compact and crystal declaration, the pastor teaches orthodox Lutheran vicarious satisfaction. He teaches Christ's active obedience (the perfect life) and his passive obedience (innocent death). He teaches the effect of Christ's substitutional obedience which is satisfaction (removed your guilt forever).

In Forde, grace and mercy always had been offered, even without the work of Christ. Our trouble is that we would not

---

[68] Gerhard O. Forde, "In Our Place," in *A More Radical Gospel*, 101-113.

[69] "Stricken, Smitten, and Afflicted," LSB 451, TLH 153, ELH 297, CW1993 127, LW 116, AH 75, ALH 399.

[70] Divine Service, Setting Three, *Lutheran Service Book* (St. Louis: Concordia Publishing House, 2006), 184.

[71] Service of the Word, *Christian Worship: A Lutheran Hymnal* (Milwaukee, Northwestern Publishing House, 1993), 38.

believe that, says Forde,[72] and the job of the cross is to convince us. On the cross, Christ did not purchase and win me as Luther says in the Catechism. Instead, the cross is how Christ reveals the grace and mercy of God, so that we will know about it and rely on it instead of on ourselves. The cross reveals a free-standing mercy that declares a general amnesty apart from anything being done to turn away the wrath of God or satisfy justice.

If you are keeping count, so far, the meanings of "Law," "Gospel," substitution, "in our place," "happy exchange," and "for Christ's sake" have been changed. David P. Scaer and Andrew Preus have shown amply that Luther's "theology of the cross" also has been given a new meaning.[73] At another time, we could continue our observations of the infiltration of the Lutheran lexicon with alien meanings. When so many core terms have double meanings, equivocation reaches a threshold of obfuscation.

Edginess Going Over the Edge

To be fair to Forde, however, sometimes his disciples go significantly beyond him. Some of their errors about Christ and the atonement should not necessarily be attributed back to their teacher.

For example, in Paulson's drive to reject the so-called "legal scheme" of the atonement, look how far he has gone to deny the obedience of Christ to the Law. In *Lutheran Theology*, while at the bottom of one page admitting that Christ is without sin,[74] at the top of the next page he launches into an elaborate indictment of Christ as having sins of his own, as

---

[72] "The problem, however, is that we could not buy that." Forde, "Caught in the Act," 26.

[73] Scaer, "Is Law Intrinsic," 3-18; and Andrew Preus, "The Theology of the Cross and the Lutheran Confessions," *Concordia Theological Quarterly*, 81:1-2, January/April 2018, 83-105.

[74] Steven D. Paulson, *Lutheran Theology* (London: T & T Clark, 2011), 104.

being "an original sinner." He speculates into unrevealed mysteries of Gethsemane putting confession of sins of his own into Christ's mouth when He prayed that the cup might pass from him. He accuses Christ of the original sin of unbelief. He portrays Christ's cry on the cross, "My God, My God, why have You forsaken Me," as faithlessness. He says,

> "Confessing made it so, and thus Christ committed his own, personal sin – not only an actual sin, but the original sin. ... He looked upon himself on the cross and believed in his own belief."[75]

He has it bass ackwards (pardon my Montanan). As David P. Scaer says:

> This bizarre and totally unacceptable interpretation cannot go unanswered. Jesus' plea to God in the moment of his greatest desperation was the most profound expression of faith ever spoken. True faith is not seen in the hour of health and prosperity but in the moment when the believer is overwhelmed by death. Jesus' enemies got it right: "He trusts in God; let God deliver him" (Matt. 27:43).[76]

Some have tried to rehabilitate this teaching by Paulson. They say, oh, he is only being edgy about Paul saying "He made Him to be sin for us" in 2 Corinthians 5:21. They say, oh, it is just an exaggerated way of speaking about imputation of sin to Jesus.

That does not work for several reasons. First, it requires omitting words from what Paul said: "He made Him *who knew no sin* to be sin for us." Second, it requires eisegesis, dragging in from outside of Paulson's text a presupposed

---

[75] Paulson, *Lutheran Theology*, 105.

[76] David P. Scaer, "Is Law Intrinsic," 14.
https://media.ctsfw.edu/Text/ViewDetails/16407.

meaning. His text, his immediate context in the paragraph, the nearby context in the chapter, and his wide context in the book *Lutheran Theology* do not allow for that exegesis of what he said. Third, and striking at the foundation of his entire theology, Paul says "sin is not imputed when there is no law." (Romans 5:13). Imputation is legal, and where there is no law, there is no imputation. When the whole project and agenda of *Lutheran Theology* is to abolish the "legal scheme," imputation is ruled out categorically *a prior*. It will not do to say, we abolish the legal scheme, but we retain bits and pieces of it convenient to defend against charges that give a proper name to accusing Christ of sin.

A thread of fideism—faith in faith—runs through the adversaries' doctrine. By relocating atonement from the cross to our consciences and our so-called faith in bloodless absolution, the adversaries lay upon us the unbearable heaviness of faith in our faith. Instead of evaluating the innocence and preciousness of the blood of Christ, their doctrine puts upon us to evaluate the quality of our faith. That quality will be wanting and hence another "monster of uncertainty," in Luther's expression. In similar fashion, we just saw Paulson say, Christ "believed in his own belief." At least their teaching can be credited at this point with a kind of consistency. In the context of the Lord's Supper, Rolf D. Preus diagnoses this:

> The denial of the vicarious satisfaction necessarily attributes to faith as it receives the blood [during the Lord's Supper] what it denies to the blood when it was shed. By rendering the atonement a mere abstraction and identifying the reconciliation in the present mystical union only, the foundation of faith is torn out from under it. Faith feeds on itself. Fideism – defined as faith in faith –

is a self-devouring process that leads to despair.[77]

That is what happens to sinners under fideism. Paulson portrays Christ as falling to the self-devouring process that leads to despair. Against Paulson's theory, the Church sings:

> Jesus, who through scourge and scorn
> Held Thy faith unshaken[78]

Separation of Justification from Atonement

One way of describing the controversy is to say that the adversaries separate justification from atonement. Robert D. Preus in his 1981 "Perennial Problems in the Doctrine of Justification" said "The second assault against the article of justification by faith is to separate God's act of justifying the sinner through faith from its basis in Christ's atonement."[79] Preus said,

> This was done already in the Middle Ages when Abelard denied the vicarious atonement, but also by the nominalists who taught that justification was indeed a forensic act of God, but made it dependent upon His will rather than the atonement and righteousness of Christ. But the same tendency to separate God's justification of the individual sinner from its basis in Christ's atoning work really pervades all Roman Catholic theology, with a few exceptions, to this very day. Luther rails incisively against this Christless soteriology.[80]

---

[77] Rolf D. Preus, "Justification," Steadfast Lutherans Conference, Zion Lutheran Church, Tomball, Texas, February 17, 2017, https://christforus.org/Justification.htm

[78] "Jesus, Name All Names Above," *Ambassador Hymnal for Lutheran Worship* (Minneapolis: The Coordinating Committee of the Association of Free Lutheran Congregations, 1994), 80.

[79] Robert D. Preus, "Perennial Problems in the Doctrine of Justification," *Concordia Theological Quarterly*, 45:3 (July 1981), 163-184, 165

[80] Preus, "Perennial Problems," 166.

Preus then adduced strident statements of Luther in which he indeed does rail against the separation of justification from the atonement. Against the error, Preus said:

> We note the close connection between the righteousness of faith, our justification, and the vicarious atonement of Christ. They entail each other. There can be no imputation of Christ's righteousness with which I can stand before God, if Christ did not by His atonement acquire such a righteousness. The purpose of Christ's vicarious work of obedience is that it might be imputed to me and all sinners. Therefore, to deny the vicarious atonement or to separate it from my personal justification threatens or vitiates the doctrine of justification by faith entirely.[81]

David P. Scaer noted the same error of separating justification from atonement in his 2008 symposium presentation "Flights from the Atonement."[82] An aspect that Scaer adds is this: the tendency to separate justification from atonement is not just a trait of the adversaries; it is a tendency of Lutherans in general. Charles A. Gieschen summarizes Scaer's article as follows:

> David Scaer addresses the tendency of Lutherans to see atonement as a doctrine easily separated from — and less important than — justification. He demonstrates the intimate interrelationship and interdependence of these doctrines as well as the current challenges being issued against a proclamation of the atonement that is faithful to the teaching of the Scriptures, especially of Jesus in the

---

[81] Preus, "Perennial Problems," 166.

[82] David P. Scaer, "Flights from the Atonement," *Concordia Theological Quarterly*, vol. 72, no. 3, 2008, pp. 195–210.

Gospels.[83]

In accord is Kleinig's 2020 symposium statement noted above that "They separate justification from its foundation in Christ's atoning death and his fulfilment of God's law by what he suffered on our behalf.[84]

The basic controversy in a nutshell is a denial of the Apology of the Augsburg Confession, Article V, paragraph 101, which confesses:

> We are justified only when we receive Christ as the Atoning Sacrifice and believe that for Christ's sake God is reconciled to us. Neither is justification even to be dreamed of without Christ as the Atonement.

Socinianism

While Socinianism might not be among the direct inspirations of modern rejections of vicarious satisfaction including Forde's, Kilcrease says "the Socinians present similar patterns of argumentation."[85]

> For Calvin, the work of Christ possessed no inherent value. Nevertheless, the Father affirmed that the death of Christ would suffice as the price of salvation by fiat, and hence it became so. Gerhard notes that in a similar manner, Calvinists also hold that God chooses the elect without reference to the merit of Christ (contrary to Eph 1:5).

> Seen from this perspective, Gerhard's insight into the Socinian position proves cogent. If God was capable of arbitrarily choosing the elect and simply

---

[83] Charles A. Gieschen, "The Death of Jesus as Atonement for Sin," *Concordia Theological Quarterly*, vol. 72, no. 3, 2008, p. 194

[84] John W. Kleinig, "Sacrificial Atonement," 195.

[85] Kilcrease, "Modern Rejections," 20.

assigning a value to the work of Christ (as Calvin and some of the Reformed authors claimed), then why should one not take this position to the extreme and claim that God can simply decree forgiveness and salvation with an equal level of arbitrariness (i.e., without the death of Christ as the price)? Indeed, it is Gerhard's contention that this is precisely what the Socinians did.[86]

Love and Blood

The adversaries say that the doctrine of vicarious satisfaction as a "legal scheme" is contrary to God's love. They say that if the penalty of the Law for sin was suffered for us by Christ, then the forgiveness of sins is not based on mercy. We saw that for example in quotations of Forde's "up and forgive" theory in "Caught in the Act." Does that fairly represent Lutheran Orthodoxy?

Consider the question, Did God's love move him to forgive sin or did the blood of Christ move God to forgive sin. Lutheran Orthodoxy answers, "Yes." Both are true. Picking one and rejecting the other is a false dichotomy. Might we agree that Who knows the answer to those two questions is Jesus himself? He says:

> For God so loved the world that He gave His only begotten Son, that whoever believes in Him should not perish but have everlasting life. For God did not send His Son into the world to condemn the world, but that the world through Him might be saved.

To the question, "Did God's love move him to forgive sin," Lutheran Orthodoxy trustingly, gratefully, and adoringly answers "Yes." Jesus himself says that "God so loved the world" that the world not be condemned but saved. Unlike fallen humanity, however, God in his love knows what love

---

[86] Kilcrease, "Modern Rejections," 32.

must do to save. God understands love better than we do. Jesus reveals here that God did not just "up and forgive" but instead, because of his love, "gave His only begotten Son." In this giving of the Son, what was the Father's will? Paul greets the churches of Galatia, saying

> Grace to you and peace from God the Father and our Lord Jesus Christ, who gave Himself for our sins, that He might deliver us from this present evil age, according to the will of our God and Father. (Galatians 1:3)

The Lord Jesus Christ gave himself for our sins according to the will of our God and Father. That is what God in his love knew love had to do for us. Jesus reveals that this was a commandment He received from his Father.

> Therefore My Father loves Me, because I lay down My life that I may take it again. No one takes it from Me, but I lay it down of Myself. I have power to lay it down, and I have power to take it again. This command I have received from My Father. (John 10:17-18)

Thus, the question, "Did the blood of Christ move God to forgive sin," Lutheran Orthodoxy also trustingly, gratefully, and adoringly answers "Yes." To deny this is a one-sided reductionism. Lutheran Orthodoxy is the full-orbed truth that teaches the "full counsel of God."

In the touching and affective scene of Paul's departure from those he so loved in Ephesus after ministering there three years, the longest of any of his missions prior to his imprisonment, he says:

> And indeed, now I know that you all, among whom I have gone preaching the kingdom of God, will see my face no more. Therefore I testify to you this day that I am innocent of the blood of all men. For I have not shunned to declare to you the whole counsel of God. Therefore take heed to yourselves

and to all the flock, among which the Holy Spirit has made you overseers, to shepherd the church of God which He purchased with His own blood. (Acts 20:25-28)

The whole counsel of God embraces that God purchased the church with his own blood. Because Paul declared the whole counsel of God including Christ's blood atonement, he is innocent of the blood of all men.

Scripture reveals the mighty acts of the Trinity – Father, Son, and Holy Spirit – in our salvation. The Father acted. The Son acted. The Holy Spirit acted. This is spread all over the pages of Scripture, but we can find it in one tidy package in a single verse:

How much more shall the blood of Christ, who through the eternal Spirit offered Himself without spot to God, cleanse your conscience from dead works to serve the living God? (Hebrews 9:14)

Christ offered his blood. God received and accepted his blood.[87] He offered it through the Spirit. Other passages ascribe the justifying resurrection of Christ (Romans 4:25) to the Father (Romans 6:4, Galatians 1:1, Acts 5:30), and to the Son (John 10:18), and to the Holy Spirit (Romans 8:11). Oversimplifying the atonement into a love-determined "up and forgive" salvation entails an oversimplification of God into a monism of so-called "love." Love then functions in Lutheran theology the way sovereignty functions in Reformed theology.

Distinction of Anselm and Luther

Earlier I said the adversaries critique Lutheran Orthodoxy's vicarious satisfaction as if it were more or less identical with

---

[87] Christ offered satisfaction not to the Father only. He offered satisfaction to the whole Godhead.

Anselm's penal substitution. A significant distinction between Anselm and Luther needs to be realized.

Luther's and Lutheran Orthodoxy's atonement is not only the penal substitution of Anselm, but the full vicarious satisfaction. As Pieper explains, Anselm's penal substitution, which is right as far as it goes, embraces the passive obedience but not the active obedience of Christ for us.

> Anselm of Canterbury declared in his book *Cur Deus Homo* (II, 11) that Christ's obedience did not form a part of the satisfaction rendered for men because Christ, as every other rational creature, owed God his obedience.[88]

Forde says, Lutheran "orthodoxy differs from Anselm in its emphasis upon active obedience in the fulfillment of the law as well as passive obedience."[89] Thus, he sometimes recognizes the distinction even if at other times he proceeds against Lutheran Orthodoxy as if the distinction did not exist.

That is not the only difference between Anselm and Luther, but it suffices for present purposes. For a thorough comparison of Anselm and Luther, see Burnell F. Eckardt, Jr.'s doctoral dissertation, *Anselm and Luther on the Atonement: Was it "Necessary"?*[90]

This difference between the "Anselmic model" and Lutheran theology has immense practical effects. Hear Luther in the

---

[88] Francis Pieper, *Christian Dogmatics*, vol. II (St. Louis: Concordia Publishing House, 1951), II.373.

[89] Gerhard O. Forde, "The Position of Orthodoxy," in Gerhard O. Forde, *The Essential Forde: Distinguishing Law and Gospel*, eds. Nicholas Hopman, Mark C. Mattes, and Steven D. Paulson (Minneapolis: Fortress Press, 2019), 39.

[90] Burnell F. Eckardt, Jr. *Anselm and Luther on the Atonement: Was it "Necessary"?* (San Francisco: Mellen Research University Press, 1992). See T. R. Halvorson, "Commentary on Burnell F. Eckardt, Jr.'s Anselm and Luther on the Atonement: Was It 'Necessary'?", https://trhalvorson.com/wp-content/uploads/2021/09/Commentary_BurnellEckardt_AnselmLutherOnAtonement.pdf

following from Pieper:

> This teaching of Scripture is of great practical
> importance. In his life of faith the Christian
> continually resorts to Christ's vicarious fulfillment
> of the Law. Luther: "He satisfied the Law; He
> fulfilled the Law perfectly, for He loved God with all
> His heart, and with all His soul, and with all His
> strength, and with all his mind, and He loved His
> neighbor as Himself. Therefore, when the Law
> comes and accuses you of not having kept it, bid it
> go to Christ. Say: There is the Man who has kept it;
> to Him I cling; He fulfilled it for me and gave his
> fulfillment to me." (Erl. XV, 611, 63.)[91]

Thus, while orthodox Lutherans ought to defend the
Anselmic position up to a point, defending Lutheran
Orthodoxy is not identical with defending Anselm. To refute
Anselm where he is errant or incomplete can be used by the
adversaries as a sleight of hand in purporting to refute
Lutheran Orthodoxy. That is a fallacy that we should not fall
into and that we should be ready to expose when the sleight
of hand is used against orthodoxy.

Vital Doctrine and Old Controversy

Vital Doctrine

Junius B. Remensnyder says that because the atonement
"directly concerns each one's personal salvation, the interest
attaching to it is not to be computed. The realization of the
significance of the atonement is the most tremendous thing
for every immortal soul."[92]

Occupying this vital place in the body of Christian

---

[91] Pieper, *Christian Dogmatics*, II.375.

[92] Junius B. Remensnyder, *The Atonement and Modern Thought* (Philadelphia:
Lutheran Publication Society, 1905) 36.

truth, it naturally is selected as a principal target of attack. So we find that against perhaps no other doctrine confessed by the whole Christian Church is there such a concert of hostile criticism as is now experienced by this one. It is either openly denied or so stated as to deprive it of any positive significance.[93]

Concurring, J. K. Mozley says "There is no Christian doctrine which arouses fiercer resentment and opposition than the subject of our present study. ... The Christian Doctrine of the Atonement marks a point at which differences ... become especially acute."[94]

At the 2019 Congress on the Lutheran Confessions, Andrew J. Preus said, "The topic assigned to me is 'The Atonement: When did Lutherans start denying it?' This is a long story, which goes back to the fall in the Garden of Eden."[95]

> The teaching that Jesus made satisfaction for sins is at the center of all Christian doctrine. Sinful man is justified before God through faith *on account of Christ* who made satisfaction for sins (AC IV). This is why we must expect the devil to attack it in every generation.[96]

Kilcrease says, "Among the many historic Christian doctrines that have received a cold reception in post-Enlightenment theology, the doctrine of substitutionary atonement stands out particularly as an object of derision."[97] He says,

---

[93] *Ibid.*

[94] J. K. Mozley, *The Doctrine of the Atonement* (New York: Charles Scribner's Sons, 1916), v.

[95] Andrew J. Preus, "The Atonement: When Did Lutherans Start Denying It?" Congress on the Lutheran Confessions, May 10, 2019.

[96] *Ibid.*

[97] Kilcrease, "' Modern Rejections," 19.

For Lutheran Christians, modern flights from substitutionary atonement are highly problematic not only because they directly contradict numerous and clear statements of the Bible and the Book of Concord but also because they endanger the chief article of Christianity: justification through faith alone. Put succinctly, without a Christ who genuinely fulfills the law on behalf of humanity (both actively and passively), there would be no alien righteousness for justifying faith to receive. As is evident from the soft moralism from the opponents of substitutionary atonement, rejection of substitutionary atonement inevitably leads to a form of works-righteousness.[98]

Old Controversy

At the 2020 symposium, Peter J. Scaer said,

Anti-atonement theology has been circulating for quite some time, with little obvious effect on the world of confessional Lutheranism. But lately, there seems to be some confusion on this subject even within confessional Lutheranism.[99]

The question whether the confusion has happened only lately bears further inquiry. Evidence from Kurt E. Marquart, Robert D. Preus, C. F. W. Walther, Francis Pieper, and others suggests that the confusion is of longer standing "in our circles" and "in our church." Maybe we just have not been smelling the coffee.

In 1961 Robert D. Preus already had said,

The last decades have witnessed some significant

---

[98] Kilcrease, "Modern Rejections," 19-20.

[99] Peter J. Scaer, "Reckoned Among the Lawless," *Concordia Theological Quarterly*, vol. 84, no. 3-4, 2020, pp. 209-225, 215.

and provocative studies in the doctrine of the Atonement. Two of these studies [by Gustaf Aulén and Karl Barth] particularly have stimulated interest by the way in which they have broken with the old Lutheran and Protestant treatment of the doctrine.[100]

In 1977, Kurt Marquart noted in *Anatomy of An Explosion: A Theological Analysis of the Missouri Synod Conflict*[101] that along with issues of Scripture, higher criticism, the confessional principle (of church fellowship), and Law-Gospel reductionism, the atonement was under attack in Seminex.

> It is no accident that von Hoffmann, who replaced both inspiration and atonement with a curious "Law/Gospel" brew of his own, is today being rediscovered by anti-traditional Lutherans in America.[102]

For his assertion Marquart cites Forde's 1969 *The Law-Gospel Debate*.[103] Look how long that was before "Caught in the Act" in 1983 and how long before the symposia in 2008 and 2020. Taking Marquart's statement and evidence in Forde's *The Law-Gospel Debate* tentatively at face value for purposes of evaluation, it purports that Law-Gospel reductionism entails a combined attack on inspiration and atonement, not just an isolated attack on inspiration. What should we think of that? Let us look at his evidence. Forde's opening paragraph in *The Law-Gospel Debate* commences thusly,

---

[100] Robert D. Preus, "The Vicarious Atonement in John Quenstedt," *Concordia Theological Monthly*, vol. xxxii, no. 2, February 1961, pp. 78-97, 78.

[101] Kurt E. Marquart, *Anatomy of an Explosion: A Theological Analysis of the Missouri Synod Conflict*, Monograph Series, number 3 (Fort Wayne, IN: Concordia Theological Seminary Press, 1977).

[102] Marquart. *Anatomy of an Explosion*, 41. Internal citations here are to the 2022 edition edited by David P. Scaer and Douglas Judisch published by Lutheran News, Inc.

[103] Gerhard O. Forde, *The Law-Gospel Debate* (Minneapolis: Augsburg Publishing House, 1969).

The beginning of the modern debate about law and gospel took the form of a controversy over the doctrine of the atonement. The controversy erupted when J. C. K. von Hoffman attacked the orthodox doctrine of vicarious satisfaction in the name of a *heilsgeschichtliche* theology.[104]

Hier, voila. Forde proceeds to treat atonement as part of the Law-Gospel debate for the rest of the book, with chapters such as "Hoffman on the Atonement," and "The Atonement Controversy." By page 137, the line has been drawn to Karl Barth and Neo-Orthodoxy, and then to the reply to Barth by Lutherans.[105] Thus, the inspiration of Scripture, higher criticism, Neo-Orthodoxy, and Law-Gospel reductionism all are woven together with the atonement. Indeed, Paulson says, "Forde first became a theologian by taking up the great and nearly unceasing debates over atonement, and he finished the same way."[106]

Marquart shows this had been coming for a long time.

Walther and Pieper already were thoroughly familiar with the kind of Luther-scholarship which, following von Hoffmann's lead, tried to pit Luther against the Lutheran Church on doctrines like inspiration, the atonement, and others. They also understood, as many today do not, that the new, re-interpreted Luther was being opposed not only to "later Orthodoxy," but to the Formula of Concord, and thus to the Lutheran Confessions themselves.[107]

---

[104] Forde, *Law-Gospel Debate*, 3.

[105] Marquart identifies one of the significant tributaries leading to Seminex as Barthian Neo-Orthodoxy, *Anatomy of an Explosion*, 78-79, 112-114, and 118-119. Marquart refers to "the Barthian penetration of the seminary" by 1959, p. 119.

[106] Paulson, "Forde Lives!" 32.

[107] Marquart, *Anatomy of an Explosion*, 46. See also Marquart's discussion of the linkage between sheer confessional subscription (an orthodoxy-by-

And again,

> Both Walther and Pieper, as we have seen, protested
> most vigorously against the Erlangen approach,
> particularly of its leading light, von Hofmann, who
> denied not only verbal inspiration, but even Christ's
> substitutionary atonement. Hofmann's radically
> unorthodox approach was recently, and most
> warmly, again *commended* by ALC theologian
> Gerhard Forde.[108]

We should not be surprised to find a nexus between the
rejection of Scripture (inspiration) and the rejection of the
atonement. Peter J. Scaer assembles a "barrage" (his term)[109]
of Scriptural passages that plainly teach vicarious satisfaction
before analyzing Forde's theology. He asks, "How does Forde
avoid the link between shed blood and forgiveness?" By
simply wiping texts from Scripture, including Christ's own
words, that plainly make the link.[110] Hear Forde's word over
God's Word (note that here we will read Forde's own words,
not Scaer's or anyone else's characterization of Forde).

> Mark 10:45 has Jesus say that the Son of Man came
> to give his life "as a ransom for many," and the
> accounts of the Last Supper speak of Jesus' blood as
> his "blood of the covenant, which is poured out for
> many for the forgiveness of sins" (Matt. 26:28).
> Such passages, in their present form at least, are
> usually regarded as having come not from Jesus
> himself but from later interpretive traditions. The
> same is true of instances where Jesus predicts his

---

constitutional-paragraph theory of the church) as rabbit's foot and openness
to denial of the atonement, the Trinity of God, and the deity of Christ, pp.
73-74.

[108] Marquart, *Anatomy of an Explosion*, 109 (emphasis in the original).

[109] Peter J. Scaer, "Reckoned Among the Lawless," 211.

[110] Peter J. Scaer, "Reckoned Among the Lawless," 218.

own death and resurrection, such as Mark 8:13ff and 9:31, and parallels in the other Synoptics.[111]

All Forde had to do for his anti-atonement theology was retro-edit God's Word and baldly claim his higher criticism is how Scripture is "usually regarded." In this he is not unlike Rudolph Bultmann.[112] Higher Criticism, Neo-Orthodoxy, Law-Gospel Reductionism, and denial of the atonement are a team of oxen pulling together in the same yoke.

Is the situation about the atonement in "in our circles" or "in our church" new? Or is it old? It goes back *at least* to Seminex if not to Bad Boll or further, and for a long time we just were not smelling the coffee. Marquart says,

> The surprising thing ... is not that the liberal invasion was finally repelled, but that it had been tolerated for so long. ... Let us look more closely at ... the ostrich-like denials on the part of Synodical officials long after the situation had become perfectly obvious.[113]

Marquart then proceeds to take that closer look going back to 1930. There was an astounding accumulation of warnings from various quarters. Lay people, pastors, and other synods gave warnings to Missouri, but various synodical communications assured that all was well, that everything was calm.

In "Flights from the Atonement," as a preliminary observation, David P. Scaer noted that some Lutherans were beginning to separate justification and the atonement. Kleinig said in the symposia that those who attack vicarious

---

[111] Gerhard O. Forde, "The Shape of Tradition," in Carl E. Braaten and Robert W. Jensen, eds., *Christian Dogmatics.* Philadelphia: Fortress Press, 1984, II.13.

[112] Rudolf Bultmann, *The Gospel of John,* trans. G. R. Beasley-Murray, R. W. N. Hoare, and J. K. Riches (Philadelphia: Fortress Press, 1974), 54-55.

[113] Marquart, *Anatomy of an Explosion,* 86.

satisfaction "separate justification from its foundation in Christ's atoning death and his fulfilment of God's law by what he suffered on our behalf."[114] We already saw above what Robert D. Preus wrote in 1961 and 1981 about separation of justification from atonement and about attacks on vicarious satisfaction by Aulén and Barth. Recall that Preus said the separation "was done already in the Middle Ages when Abelard denied the vicarious atonement." It should have been no surprise that Forde's 1983 "Caught in the Act" begins in the 12th century with Peter Abelard[115] and uses Gustaf Aulén's 1931 *Christus Victor: An Historical Study of the Three Main Types of the Idea of the Atonement.* As Francis Pieper says,

> The modern deniers of the Vicarious Satisfaction have closely followed the pattern set by Abelard (d. 1142). He taught that the Son of God came into the flesh not to satisfy the justice of God, but to give us, by His teaching and example, particularly by His death, the supreme proof of God's love and thus to awaken in us love for God; and that by exercising this love for God we are reconciled and justified. To say that God was reconciled by the blood of the innocent Christ would be, says Abelard, "cruel and unjust."[116]

Look where that leaves you. "By exercising this love for God we are reconciled and justified." Examine your love. See whether you are reconciled and justified. To the unbearable weight of believing in your belief is added the insufferable burden of believing in your love.

---

[114] Kleinig, "Sacrificial Atonement," 195.

[115] While Forde uses Abelard's criticism of penal substitution in Anselm, he levels just as strenuous a critique of Abelard's solution as he does of Anselm's. Gerhard O. Forde, "Caught in the Act: Reflections on the Work of Christ," *World in World,* 3/1 1983, 22–31, 23–24.

[116] Francis Pieper, *Christian Dogmatics,* (St. Louis: Concordia Publishing House, 1951), II.356

Rhetorical Tactics of the Adversaries

We saw earlier from Kurt Marquart that along with issues of Scripture, higher criticism, the confessional principle (of church fellowship), and Law-Gospel reductionism, the atonement was under attack in Seminex. The rhetorical tactics of the adversaries in Seminex persist as the tactics of the adversaries on the atonement today. We cannot fully explore the tactics here, but we can make the briefest of introductory sketches of four of them.

- True heirs of Luther
- Confessional subscription as rabbit's foot
- AC/Ap 4 altered and alone
- Lutheranesque language

The adversaries present themselves as the true heirs of Luther. They portray Lutheran Orthodoxy as a defection from Luther and the Lutheran confessions. This is a major proposition in Aulén's *Christus Victor*.[117] They use their distortion of Luther's "wonderful exchange" to support their claim to be his true heirs. They use a double reductionism of AC/Ap 4 as if that were true to Luther and anyone who declines the reductionism is a defector.

During Seminex, the adversaries expended a great deal of effort and spilt a goodly amount of ink on a collection of related claims about the Lutheran confessions.

- They wielded their confessional subscription as a shield against accusations of false teaching. In *Anatomy of an Explosion*, Kurt Marquart exposed the

---

[117] Even some who otherwise might not be adversaries pick it up. Jason D. Lane says, "For his [Aulén's] critique of Melanchthon and Lutheran Orthodoxy, which both veer from Luther on the atonement, see 123-33 [in Aulén's *Christus Victor*]." Lane, "That I May Be His Own," 54, n. 3. What is he saying? Is he saying that Lutheran Orthodoxy veered from Luther on the atonement, or only that Aulén's critique says so?

fallacy of that claim in his analysis of their confessional subscription "as rabbit's foot."

- They heralded the doctrine of justification in AC/Ap 4 and used their heralding as evidence of their orthodoxy. In the process, however, they altered AC/Ap 4 by reducing them to cherry-picked language that, without context, could be distorted to support their position, and they exegeted AC/Ap 4 as if the meaning need not fit with AC/Ap 3, 5, etc., to say nothing of the rest of the Book of Concord. In other words, their use of the confessions was a reductionism within a reductionism. The outer reduction was from the whole Book of Concord to just AC/Ap 4. The inner reduction was of AC/Ap 4 to the cheery-picked portions.

As noted above, in the teaching of the adversaries, the meanings of "Law," "Gospel," substitution, "in our place," "happy exchange," "for Christ's sake," and "theology of the cross" have changed. These terms sound familiar and domestic to Lutherans, but the adversaries use them as vehicles to import notions alien to Lutheran Orthodoxy.

Conclusion

Lutheran Orthodoxy confesses that Christ ended the Law for righteousness by fulfilling it in our place. The Solid Declaration says, "By this obedience God's eternal, unchangeable righteousness, revealed in the Law, has been satisfied."[118] The adversaries teach that Christ ended the Law simply by coming in the incarnation and announcing absolution.

Their bloodless absolution denies the elements of vicarious satisfaction about God's justice, his Law, Christ's substitution in our place under the Law, his active and

---

[118] SD III.57.

passive obedience for us, the imputation of our sin to him and his righteousness to us, and God's satisfaction based on the cross.

Under the teaching of the adversaries, the weight of atonement shifts from Christ bearing the sin of the world to us believing their bloodless absolution. They lay upon us the unbearable heaviness of faith in our faith instead of faith in Christ's blood. In the name of escaping "the legal scheme" they create a monstrous legalism. They teach their sole New Law: *Thou shalt believe.* Presumptively, when someone believes what they call absolution, that is faith and then atonement happens. That leaves us to evaluate the quality of our faith rather than the innocence of Christ and the preciousness of his blood.

The adversaries reject what they call "the legal framework,"[119] "the legal order" (Gustaf Aulén),[120] or "the legal scheme" (Stephen D. Paulson)[121] of the atonement. They change the meaning of the scriptural statement that "Christ is the end [*telos:* end, goal, purpose, objective] of the law" (Romans 10:4) to being a sheer termination without fulfillment. The end of the Law comes not by the blood of Christ but by the passage from one historical dispensation of Law to another historical dispensation of "Gospel."

Some of the adversaries effectively deny the active obedience of Christ by accusing him of his own sin, even the original sin of unbelief in Gethsemane and on the cross. That is how far they go to rid the atonement of "the legal scheme." Christ becomes disqualified from being the Lamb of God without blemish. Since Christ lacks his own sinless merit, there can

---

[119] Lane, "That I May Be His Own," 54.

[120] Gustaf Aulén, *Christus Victor: An Historical Study of the Three Main Types of the Idea of the Atonement*, trans. A. G. Herbert (New York: Macmillan, 1969), 91.

[121] Steven D. Paulson, *Lutheran Theology* (London: T & T Clark, 2011), pretty much the entire book.

be no imputation of his righteousness to us. Dying in his own sin, He cannot die our death for us. God's justice, God's Law, substitution, active obedience, passive obedience, imputation, and satisfaction all evaporate. With them evaporate love, mercy, salvation, and eternal life.

Chapter Two

Vicarious Satisfaction in Explanations of Luther's Small Catechism

This chapter exhibits how the Lutheran church has taught the truth of vicarious satisfaction across synods and centuries in North America in explanations of Luther's Small Catechism. With interesting variations of language, and coming originally from German, Norwegian, and English sources, they all teach the same thing.

Explanations consulted below include:

- The one used in my confirmation instruction (Grimsby, ALC)
- The one used in my father's confirmation instruction (Pontoppidan translated by Lund)
- Norwegian Synod
- General Synod
- Drewes (Synodical Conference)
- AELC
- Dell's
- Missouri Synod
- Wisconsin Synod
- Evangelical Lutheran Synod
- Association of Free Lutheran Congregations
- Church of the Lutheran Brethren
- The esteemed Reu
- The remarkable Koehler

My Confirmation Instruction (ALC)

When I was in confirmation instruction in the American Lutheran Church, the explanation of the Catechism used (Grimsby, 1941) taught this:[1]

> 8. With what has Christ redeemed you?

> With His perfect life and obedience Christ fulfilled the law in my stead.

> With His precious blood, and innocent suffering and death He paid for my sins.

Those two answers are the two main parts of vicarious satisfaction. The first is Christ's active obedience fulfilling the Law for me. The second is his passive obedience of innocent suffering and death as the Law's penalty for my sin.

My Father's Confirmation Instruction

My father, born in 1918 and confirmed in 1933, was taught the same thing in a country Norwegian Lutheran Home Missionary church.

> 166. Wherewith has Christ redeemed us?

> He has paid for our sins with His holy, precious blood, and with his innocent sufferings and death, and he has fulfilled the Law in our stead with his holy life and perfect obedience.[2]

Norwegian Synod

The Norwegian Synod taught the same thing in 1950:

---

[1] Henry P. Grimsby, *An Explanation of the Catechism* (Minneapolis: Augsburg Publishing House, 1941), 50-51.

[2] H. U. Sverdrup, *Explanation of Luther's Small Catechism*, trans (from Norwegian) E G. Lund, abridged ed. (Minneapolis: Augsburg Publishing House, 1900), 65.

137. Why was it necessary that the Son of God should become true man?

It was necessary that the Son of God should become true man, in order that he might fulfil the law and suffer punishment in man's stead.

138. Why was it necessary that our Savior should be true God?

It was necessary that our Savior should be true God, because otherwise His work could have had no atoning power.[3]

General Synod

The General Synod was teaching the same thing in 1846.

65. Why was it necessary that Christ should become man?

It was necessary that Christ should become man that he, by submitting to suffering and death could redeem us.

66. Why was it requisite that Christ should also be true God?

Christ had to be true God, in order that his redemption might have the efficacy to produce reconciliation with God.

67. By what did Christ redeem us, and produce reconciliation with God?

Christ effected reconciliation with God by his obedience unto death.

68. What did Christ fulfill in our stead?

---

[3] *Explanation of Luther's Small Catechism*, Norwegian Synod Edition (Minneapolis: Augsburg Publishing House, 1950), 54-55.

Christ in our stead yielded a perfect obedience to the whole law.

69. What did Christ take upon himself?

Christ took upon himself the guilt and punishment of our sins.

70. What did Christ suffer for us?

Christ died for us, and shed his blood for us, on the cross.[4]

The General Synod still was teaching the same thing in 1893:

189. What did Christ fulfill in our stead?

Christ in our stead rendered perfect obedience to the whole law.

190. Wherewith has Christ redeemed you?

Christ has redeemed me, a lost and condemned creature, purchased and won me from all sins, from death, and from the power of the devil; not with gold or silver, but with His holy, precious blood, and with His innocent sufferings and death.[5]

Drewes Catechism

The "Drewes Catechism" published by the Synodical Conference in 1930 teaches the same thing:

212. In what respect has Christ redeemed you from all sins?

a. Christ fulfilled the whole law for us and thus

---

[4] *Luther's Small Catechism*, 7th ed. (Baltimore: General Synod of the Lutheran Church, 1846), 28-29.

[5] *Luther's Small Catechism Developed and Explained* (Philadelphia: The United Lutheran Publication House, 1893), 59.

paid our great debt.

b. Christ bore the punishment of sin and thus cancelled the punishment.[6]

AELC

The Augustana Evangelical Lutheran Church's 1939 explanation of the Catechism teaches the same thing:

59. What is the work of Christ as High Priest?

As High Priest, Christ has fulfilled the law in our place, suffered and died for our sins, and ever lives to pray for us.[7]

Dell's *Senior Catechism*

Dell's *Senior Catechism*, was first published by The Wartburg Press in 1939, was in its 17th printing in 1955, and continued to be printed into the 1960s by assignment to Augsburg Publishing House. It teaches the same thing:

127. Why was it necessary for Christ to be both God and man?

True man He must be that He might put Himself under the law, suffer and die for our sins; true God He must be that He might thus merit for all men forgiveness of sin and life eternal.[8]

Jesus's suffering and death is called "vicarious" Atonement. A vicar is one who acts for someone else, in someone else's stead. Jesus suffered in our stead.

---

[6] Christopher Drews, *Martin Luther's Small Catechism Explained by Way of Questions and Answers* (St. Louis: Rudolph Vokening, 1930), 36.

[7] *Dr. Martin Luther's Small Catechism with Explanation*, rev. ed. (Rock Island, IL: Augustana Book Concern, 1939), 47.

[8] J. A. Dell, *Senior Catechism: Luther's Small Catechism in Question and Answer Form* (Columbus, OH: The Wartburg Press, 1939), 97.

He bore the lightning of God's wrath that we might enjoy the sunshine of God's love.[9]

Missouri Synod

In the Missouri Synod, the "blue Catechism" of 1943 teaches the same thing.[10]

129. Why was it necessary for our Savior to be true man?

It was necessary for our Savior to be true man —

A. That He might take our place under the Law.

B. That He might be able to suffer and die in our stead.

130. Why was it necessary for our Savior to be true God?

It was necessary for our Savior to be true God —

A. That His fulfilling of the Law might be sufficient for all men.

B. That His life and death might be a sufficient ransom for our redemption.

Missouri's "burgundy Catechism" of 1991 teaches the same thing:[11]

122. Why was it necessary for our Savior to be true man?

Christ had to be true man in order to

---

[9] Dell, 103.

[10] *A Short Explanation of Dr. Martin Luther's Small Catechism: A Handbook of Christian Doctrine* (St. Louis: Concordia Publishing House, 1943), rev'd 1965, 106.

[11] *Luther's Small Catechism with Explanation* (St. Louis: Concordia Publishing House, 1991), 125-125.

A. act in our place under the Law and fulfill it for us (active obedience);

B. be able to suffer and die for our guilt because we failed to keep the Law (passive obedience)

123. Why was it necessary for our Savior to be true God?

Christ had to be true God in order that

A. His fulfilling of the Law, His life, suffering, and death, might be a sufficient ransom for all people.

Missouri's newest "burgundy and black Catechism" of 2017 teaches the same thing:[12]

159. Why is it so important for us as sinners that the Son of God has become our Brother?

As our brother,

A. Jesus fulfilled our obligation to keep the Law (His active obedience);

B. Jesus suffered and died to pay the penalty of our sin (His passive obedience)

Wisconsin Synod

The Wisconsin Synod's "Kuske Catechism" of 1998 teaches the same thing:

176. Why was it necessary that Jesus be both true man and true God in one person?

176a. It was necessary that Jesus be both true man and true God in one person so that he could be under God's law and also keep it perfectly for me. (active

---

[12] Luther's Small Catechism with Explanation (St. Louis: Concordia Publishing House, 2017),

obedience)

176b. It was necessary that Jesus be both true man and true God in one person so that he could die and also ransom me by his death. (passive obedience)[13]

Evangelical Lutheran Synod

The Evangelical Lutheran Synod teaches the same thing in its explanation of the Catechism:

138. Why was it necessary for our Savior to be true man?

It was necessary for our Savior to be true man in order to

fulfill the law for us (active obedience), and

suffer and die in our place (passive obedience).

139. Why was it necessary for our Savior to be true God?

It was necessary for our savior to be true God in order that

His fulfilling the law for us, and

His suffering and dying in our place might be sufficient (vicarious atonement).[14]

---

[13] David P. Kuske, *Luther's Catechism: The Small Catechism of Dr. Martin Luther and an Exposition for Children and Adults Written in Contemporary English*, 3rd ed. (Milwaukee: Northwestern Publishing House, 1998), 156.

[14] *An Explanation of Dr. Martin Luther's Small Catechism* (Mankato, MN: Evangelical Lutheran Synod, 2001), 107.

Free Lutheran Congregations

The Association of Free Lutheran Congregations teaches the same thing in its explanation of the Catechism:

166. With what means had Christ redeemed us?

He has paid for our sins with his holy and precious blood and His innocent death, and He has fulfilled the Law in our place with His holy life and His perfect obedience.[15]

Church of the Lutheran Brethren

The "red Catechism" of the Church of the Lutheran Brethren teaches the same thing:

174. How has Christ redeemed you?

Christ has redeemed me by paying for my sins with His holy and precious blood, and with His innocent sufferings and death; and by fulfilling the law in my place by His perfect life and complete obedience.[16]

Reu Catechism

Johann Michael Reu was the author of the esteemed *Catechetics, or Theory and Practice of Religious Instruction* (Chicago: Wartburg Publishing House, 1918).

By the time it appeared in its third edition in 1931 it was a 658-page manual on the history, theory, and practice of education in the Lutheran church. Reu's *Catechetics* was the first and is still the only

---

[15] *Luther's Small Catechism with Explanation* (Minneapolis: Ambassador Publications, 2007), 76.

[16] Warren Olsen and David Rinden, eds., *An Explanation of Luther's Small Catechism* (Fergus Falls, MN: Faith and Fellowship Press, 1992).

work by an American Lutheran author which attempts to survey the whole field of sacred and secular educational theory and practice and then seeks to combine these different perspectives into a systematic, scholarly whole. First making its appearance in German in 1915, it went through three editions over the subsequent twenty-five years and was a staple in Lutheran seminaries and teacher-training institutions for two generations.[17]

Reu's 1947 explanation of the Catechism teaches the same thing:

> I was a condemned creature. God, the righteous Judge, had found me guilty and in His holy wrath had turned me over to the power of sin, death, and the devil as a well-deserved punishment. These dreadful masters held me as their prisoner and slave.
>
> God's Word tells me that Jesus took my place as my substitute and by His obedience to the Father and by His willing suffering and death earned the ransom with which He purchased my freedom.
>
> In many other places the Bible uses a different way to describe what Jesus did for me, namely that He covered up my sins with His blood so that they can no longer serve as evidence against me to condemn me.
>
> These are two different ways of saying that Jesus has by His blood changed God's righteous wrath to goodwill toward me — or that He has reconciled God — so that He will no longer permit the three cruel

---

[17] Paul I. Johnston, "Christian Education in the Thought of Johann Michael Reu," *Concordia Theological Quarterly*, vol. 58, no. 2-3, April-July 1994, pp. 93-111.

masters to punish me for my sins.[18]

Koehler Catechism

The "Koehler Catechism" of 1946 still is deemed by many to be a superior explanation of the Catechism. It used the 1943 Concordia Publishing House basic text, but then was richly supplemented by Dr. Edward W. A. Koehler. Dr. Robert Preus, President of Concordia Theological Seminary, Fort Wayne wrote the foreword to the second edition when it was brought back into print in 1981 through Concordia Theological Seminary Press. Here are Koehler's annotations in questions 129 and 130.

129. Why was it necessary for our Savior to be true man?

[Answers A and B from Missouri's blue 1943 explanation]

A. In order to save man, it was necessary for Christ to do and to suffer what man should have done and suffered; hence He had to become man that as man's Substitute He might act in man's place. Therefore He did not take on the nature of angels (Heb. 2:16), but flesh and blood, a human nature (Heb. 2:14, 16), — The Law was given to man to fulfill (192, 193). But as man is not able to render a perfect obedience (See Question 88), the Son of God was made man, and was made, or put, under the Law to fulfill it for those who were under the Law (315). To fulfill man's duties under the Law it was necessary for our Savior to become man Himself. — B. By his sins man had deserved death (196), and the justice of God demanded that this penalty be fully paid. To redeem us from the curse of

---

[18] M. Reu, *An Explanation of Dr. Martin Luther's Small Catechism Together with Four Supplements* (Columbus, OH: The Wartburg Press, 1947), 109-111.

the Law, Christ had to suffer death in our place (353). But as in His divine nature He could not die, He had to become man (316: He took on flesh and blood, became man, that He might be able to die, and through His death destroy the devil, who had the power of death).

130. Why was it necessary for our Savior to be true God?

[Answer A from Missouri's blue 1943 explanation]

A sinful man can fulfill the Law not even for himself (204), much less for another; even a saint — if there were such — could keep the Law only for himself, and his obedience would not benefit anyone else (197: "The righteousness of the righteous shall be upon him" and not another). God alone is not under the Law. Therefore our Savior had to be God in order that, being put under the Law, He might fulfill it for those who could not do so themselves, and that His obedience might be sufficient for all men. For the fact that He is God gives immeasurable value to His obedience, and assures us that He fulfilled the Law to the full satisfaction of God, who was well pleased with Him (291), and that by His vicarious obedience we are made righteous (318).

[Answer B from Missouri's blue 1943 explanation]

A sinful man must die for his own sins, and he could not die for anyone else. A sinless man — if there were such — could possibly die for one other person, but at that he could not save him, because, to remain sinless, he would have to keep the Law for himself, and could not keep it for someone else. Therefore neither sinner nor saint could give to God a sufficient ransom for his brother (317). In order, then, that the suffering and death of our Redeemer might be a sufficient ransom, payment, to atone for the sins of all men (319), it was necessary for Him to be more than man, more than a saint, He had to be God. Only God can pay a ransom unto Himself (2 Cor. 5, 19). The saving value and strength of Christ's suffering and death lies not in its duration and intensity, but rather in this that it was God, who, in His human nature, suffered in Gethsemane and died on Calvary. ... The fact, then, that the *Son of God* paid the penalty of our guilt assures us that He fully satisfied the demands of divine justice against us, and that His suffering and death was a sufficient ransom for our redemption.[19]

---

[19] Edward W. A. Koehler, *A Short Explanation of Dr. Martin Luther's Small Catechism*, 2nd ed. (Fort Wayne, IN: Concordia Theological Seminary Press, 1981), 143-144.

Chapter Three

Vicarious Satisfaction in the Lutheran Confessions

This chapter shows the confession of vicarious satisfaction in the Lutheran confessions. The confessions are contained in the *Book of Concord*. For those not already familiar with it, this chapter concludes with a brief description of the *Book of Concord*.

This compendium of excerpts from the Lutheran confessions is by no means comprehensive. The confessions are shot through with vicarious satisfaction in places where it might not at first seem obvious. For example, Apology Article V has many passages explaining that because Christ is an "Atoning Sacrifice" and "Mediator" we have a "reconciled God." These terms and phrases are so compact that unless one already has seen how the confessions use them, it easily could escape notice that this is speaking of vicarious satisfaction. If all such passages had been included here, one would be reading here a significant fraction of the *Book of Concord*.

Unless otherwise noted, quotations are from Paul Timothy McCain, ed. *Concordia: The Lutheran Confessions*, 2nd ed. (St. Louis: Concordia Publishing House, 2006).

Augsburg Confession

AC III.2b-3

> There is one Christ, true God and true man, who was born of the Virgin Mary, truly suffered, was crucified, died, and was buried. [3] He did this to reconcile the Father to us and to be a sacrifice, not only for original guilt, but also for all actual sins of mankind [John 1:29].

AC IV.2-3

[2] People are freely justified for Christ's sake, through faith, when they believe that they are received into favor and that their sins are forgiven for Christ's sake. By His death, Christ made satisfaction for our sins. [3] God counts this faith for righteousness in His sight (Romans 3 and 4 [3:21–26; 4:5]).

AC XXIV.24-27

[24] Our teachers have warned that these opinions depart from the Holy Scripture and diminish the glory of the passion of Christ. [25] For Christ's passion was an offering and satisfaction, not only for original guilt, but also for all other sins, as it is written, [26] "We have been sanctified through the offering of the body of Jesus Christ once for all" (Hebrews 10:10). [27] Also, "By a single offering He has perfected for all time those who are being sanctified" (Hebrews 10:14). ‹It is an unheard-of innovation in the Church to teach that by His death Christ has made satisfaction only for original sin and not for all other sin. So it is hoped that everybody will understand that this error has been rebuked for good reason.›

Apology of the Augsburg Confession

Ap III.52

Christ suffered and died to reconcile the Father to us, and was raised again to reign, to justify, and to sanctify believers according to the Apostles' Creed and the Nicene Creed.

Ap IV.53

[53] Whenever we speak of justifying faith, we must keep in mind that these three objects belong

together: the promise, grace, and Christ's merits as the price and atonement. The promise is received through faith. Grace excludes our merits and means that the benefit is offered only through mercy. Christ's merits are the price, because there must be a certain atonement for our sins.

Ap IV.57

[57] Throughout the Prophets and the Psalms this worship (this *latreia*) is highly praised, even though the Law does not teach the free forgiveness of sins. The Old Testament Fathers knew the promise about Christ, that God for Christ's sake wanted to forgive sins. They understood that Christ would be the price for our sins. They knew that our works are not a price for so great a matter. So they received free mercy and forgiveness of sins by faith, just as the saints in the New Testament.

Ap V.57-58

[57/178] Christ's death and satisfaction ought to be placed far above our purity, far above the Law itself. This truth ought to be set before us so that we can be sure of this: We have a gracious God because of Christ's satisfaction and not because of our fulfilling the Law.

[58/179] Paul teaches this in Galatians 3:13, when he says, "Christ redeemed us from the curse of the law by becoming a curse for us." This means that the Law condemns all people. But Christ—without sin—has borne the punishment of sin. He has been made a victim for us and has removed that right of the Law to accuse and condemn those who believe in Him. He Himself is the Atonement for them. For His sake they are now counted righteous. Since they are counted righteous, the Law cannot accuse or condemn them, even though they have not actually satisfied the Law. Paul writes the same way to the Colossians, "You have been filled in Him" (2:10). This is like saying, "Although you are still far from the perfection of the Law, the remnants of sin do not condemn you. For Christ's sake we have a sure and firm reconciliation, if you believe, even though sin dwells in your flesh."

Ap V.101

We are justified only when we receive Christ as the Atoning Sacrifice and believe that for Christ's sake God is reconciled to us. Neither is justification even to be dreamed of without Christ as the Atonement.

Ap V.261

For Christ is an Atoning Sacrifice, as Paul says, "by faith" (Romans 3:25). When fearful consciences are comforted by faith, and are convinced that our sins have been blotted out by Christ's death, and that God has been reconciled to us because of Christ's suffering, then, indeed, Christ's suffering profits us.

Ap XX.82

One who knows why Christ has been given to us, and who knows that Christ is the Atoning Sacrifice for our sins, needs no further proof. Isaiah says, "The Lord has laid on Him the iniquity of us all (53.6)." The adversaries, on the other hand, teach that God does not lay our offense on Christ, but on our works.

Ap XXI.19-20

[19] The second requirement for an atonement maker is that his merits are shown to make satisfaction for other people. They are divinely given to others, so that through them, just as by their own

merits, other people may be regarded righteous. For example, when any friend pays a debt for a friend, the debtor is freed by the merit of another, as though it were by his own. So Christ's merits are given to us so that, when we believe in Him, we may be regarded righteous by our confidence in Christ's merits as though we had merits of our own.

[20] From both of these—the promise and the giving of merits—arises confidence in mercy. Such confidence in the divine promise, and likewise in Christ's merits, should be promoted when we pray. For we should be truly confident, both that for Christ's sake we are heard and that by His merits we have a reconciled Father.

Ap XIIb.43

[43/140] Besides, Christ's death is a satisfaction not only for guilt, but also for eternal death, according to Hosea 13:14, "O Death, where are your plagues?" It is freakish to say that the satisfaction of Christ redeemed from the guilt, but our punishments redeem from eternal death.

Ap XXI.22-23

[22] Second, they apply the saints' merits, just as Christ's merits, to others. They ask us to trust in the saints' merits as though we were regarded righteous because of their merits, just as we are regarded righteous by Christ's merits. We are making none of this up. [23] In indulgences, the adversaries say that they apply the saints' merits. And Gabriel Biel, the interpreter of the canon of the Mass, confidently declares, "According to the order instituted by God, we should betake ourselves to the aid of the saints, in order that we may be saved by their merits and vows." These are Gabriel's words. Nevertheless, still more silly things are read here and there in the

adversaries' books and sermons. What is this other than creating people who make atonement? If we must trust that we are saved by their merits, they are made completely equal to Christ.

Ap XXIV.22

[22] In fact there has been only one atoning sacrifice in the world, namely, Christ's death, as the Epistle to the Hebrews teaches, "It is impossible for the blood of bulls and goats to take away sins" (10:4). A little later, of the will of Christ, "By that will we have been sanctified through the offering of the body" (10:10). [23] Isaiah interprets the Law, so that we may know Christ's death is truly a satisfaction for our sins, or remedy, and that the ceremonies of the Law are not. He says, "When his soul makes an offering for sin, he shall see his offspring," and so on (Isaiah 53:10). The word used here means a victim for transgression (*asham*). In the Law this illustrated that a certain Victim was to come to make satisfaction for our sins and reconcile God. This was so that people might know that God wishes to be reconciled to us, not because of our own righteousnesses, but because of another's merits: Christ.

Ap XXIV.23b-24

Isaiah and Paul, therefore, mean that Christ became a victim, that is, a remedy, that by His merits, and not by our own, God might be reconciled. [24] Let this remain the case: Christ's death alone is truly an atoning sacrifice. For the Levitical atoning sacrifices were so called only to illustrate a future remedy. Because of a certain resemblance they were satisfactions delivering the righteousness of the Law and preventing those persons who sinned from being excluded from the commonwealth. But after the revelation of the

Gospel, those sacrifices had to end. Since they had to end in the revelation of the Gospel, they were not true atoning sacrifices, for the Gospel was promised specifically to present an atoning sacrifice.

Ap XXIV.53-56

[53] The main proofs for our belief are in the Epistle to the Hebrews. Yet, the adversaries twist mutilated passages from this Epistle against us, as in this very passage, where it is said that every high priest is ordained to offer sacrifices for sins. Scripture immediately adds that Christ is the High Priest (Hebrews 5:5-6, 10). The preceding words speak about the Levitical priesthood and show that the Levitical priesthood was an image of Christ's priesthood. The Levitical sacrifices for sins did not merit the forgiveness of sins before God. They were only an image of Christ's sacrifice, which was to be the one atoning sacrifice, as we said before. [54] To a great extent the Epistle speaks about how the ancient priesthood and the ancient sacrifices were set up not to merit the forgiveness of sins before God or reconciliation, but only to illustrate the future sacrifice of Christ alone. [55] In the Old Testament, saints had to be justified by faith, which receives the promise of the forgiveness of sins granted for Christ's sake, just as saints are also justified in the New Testament. From the beginning of the world all saints had to believe that Christ would be the promised offering and satisfaction for sins, as Isaiah 53:10 teaches, "when His soul makes an offering for sin."

[56] In the Old Testament, sacrifices did not merit reconciliation, except as a picture (for they merited civil reconciliation), but they illustrated the coming sacrifice. This means that Christ is the only sacrifice applied on behalf of the sins of others.

Therefore, in the New Testament, no sacrifice is left to be applied for the sins of others, except the one sacrifice of Christ upon the cross.

Smalcald Articles

SA II.i.1–5

As Lutherans we are accustomed to hearing, justification is the article on which the church stands or falls. As Robert Preus[1] and David Scaer[2] teach, Lutherans often make a mistake of separating justification from atonement. Notice here in the Smalcald Articles how Luther joins atonement, including vicarious satisfaction, with justification and says that this entire united truth is necessary to believe, that everything we teach depends on it, otherwise all is lost and the pope, the devil, and all adversaries win the victory and right over us.

The first and chief article is this:

[1] Jesus Christ, our God and Lord, died for our sins and was raised again for our justification (Romans 4:24–25).

---

[1] Robert D. Preus, "Perennial Problems in the Doctrine of Justification," *Concordia Theological Quarterly*, 45:3 (July 1981). "In his essay, 'Perennial Problems in the Doctrine of Justification,' Preus lists five ways in which the doctrine of justification is threatened, of which, "The second assault against the article of justification by faith is to separate God's act of justifying the sinner through faith from its basis in Christ's atonement." . . . 'There can be no imputation of Christ's righteousness with which I can stand before God, if Christ did not by His atonement acquire such righteousness.' . . . For Preus, 'The *propter Christum* is exclusive in that it is the only basis for God's verdict of justification." David P. Scaer, "Justification in the Theology of Robert D. Preus," *Concordia Theological Quarterly*, 86:1 (2022), 43-56, 51.

[2] David P. Scaer, "Flights from Atonement," *Concordia Theological Quarterly*, vol. 72, no. 3, 2008, pp. 195-210. Scaer "addresses the tendency of Lutherans to see atonement as a doctrine easily separated from – and less important than – justification. He demonstrates the intimate interrelationship and interdependence of these doctrines." Charles A. Gieschen, "The Death of Jesus as Atonement for Sin," editorial introduction to *Concordia Theological Quarterly*, vol. 72, no. 3, 2008.

[2] He alone is the Lamb of God who takes away the sins of the world (John 1:29), and God has laid upon Him the iniquities of us all (Isaiah 53:6).

[3] All have sinned and are justified freely, without their own works or merits, by His grace, through the redemption that is in Christ Jesus, in His blood (Romans 3:23–25).

[4] This is necessary to believe. This cannot be otherwise acquired or grasped by any work, law, or merit. Therefore, it is clear and certain that this faith alone justifies us. As St. Paul says:

> For we hold that one is justified by faith apart from works of the law. (Romans 3:28)

> That He might be just and the justifier of the one who has faith in Jesus. [Romans 3:26]

[5] Nothing of this article can be yielded or surrendered, even though heaven and earth and everything else falls [Mark 13:31].

> For there is no other name under heaven given among men by which we must be saved. (Acts 4:12)

> And with His stripes we are healed. (Isaiah 53:5)

Upon this article everything that we teach and practice depends, in opposition to the pope, the devil, and the whole world. Therefore, we must be certain and not doubt this doctrine. Otherwise, all is lost, and the pope, the devil, and all adversaries win the victory and the right over us.

SA III.iii.38

[38] Neither can the satisfaction be uncertain, because it is not our uncertain, sinful work. Rather,

it is the suffering and blood of the innocent Lamb of God, who takes away the sin of the world [John 1:29].

Large Catechism

LC II.31

Let this then be the sum of this article: the little word *Lord* means simply the same as *redeemer*. It means the One who has brought us from Satan to God, from death to life, from sin to righteousness, and who preserves us in the same. But all the points that follow in this article serve no other purpose than to explain and express this redemption. They explain how and by whom it was accomplished. They explain how much it cost Him and what He spent and risked so that He might win us and bring us under His dominion. It explains that He became man [John 1:14], was conceived and born without sin [Hebrews 4:15], from the Holy Spirit and from the virgin Mary [Luke 1:35], so that He might overcome sin. Further, it explains that He suffered, died, and was buried so that He might make satisfaction for me and pay what I owe [1 Corinthians 15:3–4], not with silver or gold, but with His own precious blood [1 Peter 1:18–19]. And He did all this in order to become my Lord. He did none of these things for Himself, nor did He have any need for redemption. After that He rose again from the dead, swallowed up and devoured death [1 Corinthians 15:54], and finally ascended into heaven and assumed the government at the Father's right hand [1 Peter 3:22]. He did these things so that the devil and all powers must be subject to Him and lie at His feet [Hebrews 10:12–13] until finally, at the Last Day, He will completely divide and separate us from the wicked world, the devil, death, sin, and such [Matthew 25:31–46; 13:24–30, 47–50].

LC IV.37

[37] So you see plainly that there is no work done here by us, but a treasure, which God gives us and faith grasps [Ephesians 2:8–9]. It is like the benefit of the Lord Jesus Christ upon the cross, which is not a work, but a treasure included in the Word. It is offered to us and received by faith.

Formula of Concord: Epitome

Ep III.3

[3] 1. Against both the errors just mentioned, we unanimously believe, teach, and confess that Christ is our Righteousness [1 Corinthians 1:30] neither according to His divine nature alone nor according to His human nature alone. But it is the entire Christ who is our Righteousness according to both natures. In His obedience alone, which as God and man He offered to the Father even to His death [Philippians 2:8], He merited for us the forgiveness of sins and eternal life. For it is written, "For as by the one man's disobedience the many were made sinners, so by the one man's obedience the many will be made righteous" (Romans 5:19).

Formula of Concord: Solid Declaration

SD III.4

[4] In opposition to both these groups it has been unanimously taught by the other teachers of the Augsburg Confession that Christ is our righteousness not according to His divine nature alone, nor according to His human nature alone, but according to both natures. For He has redeemed, justified, and saved us from our sins as God and man, through His complete obedience. Therefore, the righteousness of faith is the forgiveness of sins,

reconciliation with God, and our adoption as God's children only on account of Christ's obedience. Christ's obedience alone—out of pure grace—is credited for righteousness through faith alone to all true believers. They are absolved from all their unrighteousness by this obedience.

SD III.9–16

[9] We unanimously believe, teach, and confess the following about the righteousness of faith before God, in accordance with the comprehensive summary of our faith and confession presented above. A poor sinful person is justified before God, that is, absolved and declared free and exempt from all his sins and from the sentence of well-deserved condemnation, and is adopted into sonship and inheritance of eternal life, without any merit or worth of his own. This happens without any preceding, present, or subsequent works, out of pure grace, because of the sole merit, complete obedience, bitter suffering, death, and resurrection of our Lord Christ alone. His obedience is credited to us for righteousness.

[10] These treasures are brought to us by the Holy Spirit in the promise of the Holy Gospel. Faith alone is the only means through which we lay hold on, accept, apply, and take them for ourselves. [11] This faith is God's gift [Ephesians 2:8–9], by which we truly learn to know Christ, our Redeemer, in the Word of the Gospel and trust in Him. We trust that for the sake of His obedience alone we have the forgiveness of sins by grace, are regarded as godly and righteous by God the Father, and are eternally saved. [12] Therefore, it is considered and understood to be the same thing when Paul says (a) we are "justified by faith" (Romans 3:28) or (b) "faith is counted as righteousness" (Romans 4:5)

and when he says (c) "by the one man's obedience the many will be made righteous" (Romans 5:19) or (d) "so one act of righteousness leads to justification and life for all men" (Romans 5:18). [13] Faith justifies not because it is such a good work or because it is so beautiful a virtue. It justifies because it lays hold of and accepts Christ's merit in the promise of the Holy Gospel. For this merit must be applied and become ours through faith, if we are to be justified by it. [14] Therefore, the righteousness that is credited to faith or to the believer out of pure grace is Christ's obedience, suffering, and resurrection, since He has made satisfaction for us to the Law and paid for <expiated> our sins. [15] Christ is not man alone, but God and man in one undivided person. Therefore, He was hardly subject to the Law (because He is the Lord of the Law), just as He didn't have to suffer and die for His own sake. For this reason, then, His obedience (not only in His suffering and dying, but also because He was voluntarily made under the Law in our place and fulfilled the Law by this obedience) is credited to us for righteousness. So, because of this complete obedience, which He rendered to His heavenly Father for us by doing and suffering and in living and dying, God forgives our sins. He regards us as godly and righteous, and He eternally saves us. [16] This righteousness is brought to us by the Holy Spirit through the Gospel and in the Sacraments. It is applied, taken, and received through faith. Therefore, believers have reconciliation with God, forgiveness of sins, God's grace, sonship, and are heirs of eternal life.

SD III.25

[25] Not everything that belongs to conversion also belongs to the article of justification. Only God's grace, Christ's merit, and faith belong and are

necessary to the article of justification. Faith receives these blessings in the promise of the Gospel, by which Christ's righteousness is credited to us. From this we receive and have forgiveness of sins, reconciliation with God, sonship, and are made heirs of eternal life.

SD III.56-58

[56] Even if Christ had been conceived and born without sin by the Holy Spirit and had fulfilled all righteousness in His human nature alone, and yet had not been true and eternal God, this obedience and suffering of His human nature could not be credited to us for righteousness. Also, if God's Son had not become man, the divine nature alone could not be our righteousness. Therefore, we believe, teach, and confess that the entire obedience of Christ's entire person (which He has offered to the Father for us, even to His most humiliating death on the cross) is credited to us for righteousness. For the human nature alone, without the divine, could not by obedience or suffering make satisfaction to eternal, almighty God for the sins of all the world. However, the divinity alone, without the humanity, could not mediate between God and us.

[57] As mentioned above, the obedience not only of one nature, but of the entire person, is a complete satisfaction and atonement for the human race. By this obedience God's eternal, unchangeable righteousness, revealed in the Law, has been satisfied. So our righteousness benefits us before God and is revealed in the Gospel. Faith relies on this before God, which God credits to faith, as it is written in Romans 5:19:

> For as by the one man's disobedience the many were made sinners, so by the one man's obedience the many will be made righteous.

The blood of Jesus His Son cleanses us from all sin. (1 John 1:7)

The righteous shall live by his faith. (Habakkuk 2:4 [see also Romans 1:17])

[58] Neither Christ's divine nor human nature by itself is credited to us for righteousness, but only the obedience of the person who is at the same time God and man. And faith thus values Christ's person because it was made under the Law [Galatians 4:4] for us and bore our sins, and, in His going to the Father, He offered to His heavenly Father for us poor sinners His entire, complete obedience. This extends from His holy birth even unto death. In this way, He has covered all our disobedience, which dwells in our nature, and its thoughts, words, and works. So disobedience is not charged against us for condemnation. It is pardoned and forgiven out of pure grace alone, for Christ's sake.

Book of Concord

The Lutheran church published its confessions in the *Book of Concord* (1580). Pastors in confessional synods subscribe to the *Book of Concord* without qualification because it is a correct exposition of what Scripture reveals about the faith.

The confessions include eight parts:

1. Three Chief Symbols (Apostles, Nicene, and Athanasian Creeds)
2. Augsburg Confession (1530)
3. Apology of the Augsburg Confession (1531)
4. Smalcald Articles (1537)
5. Treatise on the Power and Primacy of the Pope (1537)
6. Small Catechism (1529)
7. Large Catechism (1529)
8. Formula of Concord (1577)

The Creeds were formulated long before the Reformation. They were formulated before corruptions of the Gospel that had come into the Church in the last roughly 200 to 300 years before the Reformation. The Lutheran church confesses the Creeds in accord with the early Christians.

During the Reformation, the Holy Roman Emperor summoned an imperial meeting at Augsburg. Each party was commanded to give its confession of faith. The stated purpose was to identify areas where the parties could agree and thereby reduce the areas of dispute, but also to state what articles of faith were in real dispute so that, optimistically, those could be addressed later. The Lutherans appeared and read to the Emperor their *Augsburg Confession*.

The *Apology* or *Defense of the Augsburg Confession* replies to an unpublished *Confutation* of the Roman church against the *Augsburg Confession*.

The *Smalcald Articles* are a confession of faith by Martin Luther setting forth what, at a later time, sill remained nonnegotiable articles of faith.

The *Treatise* addresses the offices of pope, bishop, and pastor-elder-bishop both in Scripture and by human arrangement.

Martin Luther wrote the *Small Catechism* for the instruction of lay people. Many years, much study, much preaching, and many decisions about options on how to teach the "six chief parts of Christian doctrine" went into the drafting. The result can be understood by children, and yet in lifelong study never can be fully mastered by elder adults or doctors of the church. The six parts are the Ten Commandments, Apostles' Creed, Lord's Prayer, Baptism, Confession and Absolution, Sacrament of the Altar, and Table of Duties. Also included are morning and evening prayers and grace at table.

Martin Luther wrote the *Large Catechism* to show pastors and teachers how to teach the faith, but again, he did this in such a plain style that anyone can understand it.

Martin Luther died in 1543. Without his unifying influence, controversies arose in the Lutheran churches. The *Formula of Concord* resolved many of the controversies in 1577.

With the confession of the *Formula of Concord*, the Lutheran pastors and theologians drew together what they recognized as the confessions of the Lutheran church into the *Book of Concord* (1580).

In English there are several popular editions of the *Book of Concord* that go by the following abbreviated names:

- Tappert
- Concordia or McCain
- Kolb & Wengert
- Triglotta

Chapter Four

Vicarious Satisfaction in Lutheran Hymns

Introduction

Lutheran hymns have a special characteristic as confessions of the faith. That makes them witnesses to authentic Lutheran doctrine. This chapter recites an abundance of evidence from the texts of Lutheran hymns confessing vicarious satisfaction.

As prolegomena to that recitation, this chapter first presents a background about:

- The eruption of Lutheran hymns
- The character of Lutheran hymns as confessions of the faith
- What Lutheran hymns confess
- Difficulties of the study of the hymns regarding vicarious satisfaction
- A definition of the body of hymns reviewed
- The criteria for identification of lyrics that confess vicarious satisfaction derived from the formulation of the doctrine of vicarious satisfaction stated in Chapter One of this book
- A realization of the language of vicarious satisfaction in hymns based on that formulation
- Application of the criteria to the texts of hymns is illustrated by examples with commentary

With the criteria having been established, a sampling of the abundant evidence from the texts of Lutheran hymns is recited. Selected for recitation are explicit and brief excerpts from 58 hymns, explicit and extended excerpts from 35 hymns, and implicit excerpts from 5 hymns.

Background

An Eruption of Lutheran Hymns

"The sudden bursting forth of the Lutheran chorale is one of the most thrilling chapters in the history of the Reformation."[1] "Wherever the Reformation gained entrance, publishers vied in bringing out better and more comprehensive hymnals. Magdeburg, Zwickau, Leipzig, Erfurt, Nürnberg, Augsburg, Königsberg, and many other cities produced their own collections."[2] "The Reformation produced close to one hundred hymnals from 1524 until Luther's death in 1546."[3] "In comparison, the English Reformation produced thirteen hymnals up to the end of the sixteenth century (Scottish hymnals included)."[4]

"A book with Lutheran hymns was sure to sell, for the chorales were the fanfare that opened many a Jericho to the advent of the Reformation."[5]

> A chronicler of the city of Magdeburg gives a vivid account of a peddler who on May 6, 1524, sang the new Lutheran hymns on the marketplace and sold the leaflets to the people. The mayor had him clapped in jail, but the enthusiastic burghers saw that he was freed in short order to continue singing the hymns of Martin Luther.[6]

---

[1] Ulrich S. Leupold, "Introduction" to "The Hymns," *Luther's Works* (Philadelphia: Fortress Press, 1965), 53:191.

[2] Leupold, *op cit.*, 193.

[3] Leupold, *op cit.* 194.

[4] *Ibid*, n. 25.

[5] Leupold, *op cit.*, 195.

[6] Leupold, op cit., 191.

Lutheran Hymns Are Confessions of the Faith

It is not a stretch to class Lutheran hymns along with the Lutheran confessions and explanations of Luther's *Small Catechism* as witnesses to the doctrine of the Lutheran church. Granted, the confessions and catechism rank before the hymns, but along with the liturgy, Lutheran hymns are witnesses of the next highest rank.

In *Lutheran Service Book: Companion to the Hymns*, Richard Resch contributes the essay, "Hymns as Sung Confession." He says:

> Lutherans could rightly define the hymn as "a sung confession of the faith," for it describes what they have required of their hymns from those first days of the Reformation.[7]

> The word "confession" (as creed) fits this concise definition of a hymn so well, and it suggests this significant result: that Lutherans believe what a hymn puts onto their lips and into their hearts.[8]

> Lutheran singing preeminently confesses *the* faith (*fides quae*). The sung confession of the individual Christian, *my* faith by which I believe (*fides qua*), is secondary.[9]

> Every hymn by Luther conveys the faith. One would expect this didactic approach in his catechism hymns, but the same catechetical style continues in his psalm hymns, canticle hymns, liturgical hymns, and even his children's hymns.[10]

---

[7] Richard Resch, "Hymns as Sung Confession," *Lutheran Service Book: Companion to the Hymns* (St Louis, Concordia Publishing House, 2019), II.131.

[8] *Ibid.*

[9] *Ibid.*

[10] Resch, *op cit.*, 133.

> The didactic hymn modeled by the Wittenberg hymnists dominated Lutheran hymn writing for more than a century and a half. This sung confession consistently proclaimed Christ, his work, and His saving benefits received by His people through faith, not the individual singer and his experience. The period of orthodox Lutheran hymnody gave the Church thousands of hymns that objectively teach the faith.[11]

Ulrich S. Leupold in "Introduction" to "The Hymns," in the American Edition of *Luther's Works* says, "Luther's hymns were meant not to create a mood, but to convey a message. They were a confession of faith, not of personal feelings."[12]

Carl F. Schalk says the church's song "is a song in which proclamation, teaching, and praise interweave in a tapestry of music unique to the Church."[13]

Herman Sasse explains the essence of a church confession as bearing witness to objective truths.

> The essence of a church confession lies, first of all, in the fact that it bears witness to *objective* truths. These, like the incarnation of Christ, cannot be derived from subjective experiences and are independent of all subjective opinions. Second, it belongs to the nature of such a confession that it is the creed of the *church*, that it is confessed not only as an *I* but as a *we*.[14]

Robin A. Leaver speaks of the catechetical intentions of

---

[11] Resch, *op cit.*, 134

[12] Leupold, *op cit.*, 197

[13] Carl F. Schalk, "The Church's Song: Proclamation, Pedagogy, and Praise," *Lutheran Service Book: Companion to the Hymns* (St Louis, Concordia Publishing House, 2019), II.123.

[14] Hermann Sasse, *We Confess Jesus Christ*, trans. Norman Nagel (St. Louis: Concordia Publishing House, 1984), 74.

Lutheran hymns.

> It is because the classic Lutheran hymns were Scripture-based that they functioned not only as worship songs, expressing the response of faith to be sung within a liturgical context, but also as theological songs, declaring the substance of the faith to be sung with catechetical intensions.[15]

That we should look to our hymns to combat the error of the adversaries against vicarious satisfaction is nothing new. On the contrary, not to look to our hymns would be an abandonment of one of their uses throughout church history. "Early in its history the song of the Church, as it developed in both East and West, became a vehicle for combating error and heresy."[16] Gnosticism in the East and Arianism in the West from the second to fourth centuries immediately were combatted in hymns. Basil, Ambrose, Luther, and others extol the use of hymns to teach pure doctrine and guard against error.

> Throughout its history, the song of the Church has been a guardian of the proclamation of the Gospel. It is the Church's song that has often had to carry the story of salvation despite bad preaching or no preaching at all, despite bad liturgy or no liturgy at all.[17]

What Do Lutheran Hymns Confess?

What do Lutheran hymns confess? Carl F. Schalk shows that they do what Christian hymns always have done in continuity with the hymns of the Old and New Testaments. They proclaim the mighty acts of God. They are vivid, historical,

---

[15] Robin A. Leaver, *Luther's Liturgical Music: Principles and Implications* (Grand Rapids, Mich.: Eerdmans, 2007), 107–108.

[16] Schalk, *op cit.*, 127.

[17] Schalk, *op cit.*, 129.

and dramatic. They are not metaphysical or rationalistic. They are about what God *has done*.[18] With the coming of Christ and his work, "The song of the Church is a fruit of saving faith created by the Spirit in response to what God *has done in Jesus Christ*."[19]

That being so, the question, what *has* God done in Jesus Christ is of the essence of Lutheran hymns.

> The very first hymn in the earliest Lutheran collection of 1524, Luther's 'Dear Christians, one and all, rejoice' (*LSB* 556,) underscores this point: . . . 'Proclaim the wonders God *has done*.[20]

Along with *Christus Victor* and ransom (which Lutheran hymns clearly and abundantly sing), do Lutheran hymns sing vicarious substitution? Do they teach and confess that God laid our sin upon Christ as our substitute so that when He died, that was a stroke of justice under the Law? Do Lutherans sing that the sufferings and death of Christ were the just penalty of the Law for our sin? Do our hymns confess that Christ's suffering in our place exhausted on our behalf the penalty of death, reversed the verdict of the Law that had stood against us, freed us from condemnation, and effected our justification?

As a foreshadowing, consider this lyric: "But the deepest stroke that pierced Him was the stroke that justice gave," ("Stricken, Smitten, and Afflicted," LSB 451:2, TLH 153:2, ELH 297:2, CW1993 127:2, LW 116:2, ALH 399:2). This lyric all by itself entirely refutes the errant doctrine of the adversaries such as Gustaf Aulén, Gerhard O. Forde, and Stephen D. Paulson. In their rejection of "the legal framework" or "the legal scheme" of the atonement, they deny that once Christ

---

[18] Schalk, *op cit.*, 123-129.

[19] Schalk, *op cit.*, 123, emphasis added.

[20] Schalk, *op cit.*, 125, (emphasis added). The hymn also is in *ELH* 378, *CW1996* 377, *CW 2021* 557, *TLH* 187.

became sin for us, his death was justice under the Law, just as, had we no substitute, our deaths would be justice under the Law. But in this hymn, Thomas Kelly gives us words to confess and teach one another that not only did Jesus suffer a stroke of justice, but that it was the deepest stroke. It was deeper than the miseries of Jesus' arrest, desertions, denials, mocking, scourging, beating, sleep deprivation, false accusations, illegal trials, miscarried verdicts of the mob, Pilate, and Herod, carrying the cross beam, degradation rituals attendant to Roman crucifixion, nails, exsanguination, exposure, shock, and asphyxia.

Those all were bad, "But the deepest stroke that pierced Him was the stroke that justice gave." The adversaries deny the deepest stroke and thus deny Jesus' deepest love for us that moved him to suffer that deepest stroke in our place, thus sparing us from it. "Greater love has no one than this, than to lay down one's life for his friends." (John 15:13)

Method Used in this Study

Difficulties of this Study

Surveying the confession of vicarious satisfaction in the Lutheran confessions of the *Book of Concord* is relatively easy. Being familiar with the confessions, we already know off the tops of our heads where first to look to see how they confess the atonement. Added to that are aids in the tables of contents and indexes such as in the reader's edition published by Concordia Publishing House. The dogmatics texts such as Pieper[21] cite the confessions and point to where they confess vicarious satisfaction.

Surveying the teaching of vicarious satisfaction in explanations of the *Small Catechism* is even easier. The explanations are organized pedagogically and didactically (if

---

[21] Francis Pieper, *Christian Dogmatics* (St. Louis: Concordia Publishing House, 1950).

not systematically), and we only must flip a few pages to find the material teaching the atonement.

By comparison, surveying how Lutherans sing the atonement in hymns is much more difficult. There are multiple layers of difficulty. Following are some of them.

The corpus of hymns well used by Lutherans both currently and in prior times is vast. The universe of data is orders of magnitude greater than the explanations of the Catechism.

In English, a large fraction of the hymns are translations. Comparing a single hymn in various English hymnals shows alternative ways translators conveyed the original text with meter, length of clauses, and rhyme. Sometimes the original German or Latin clearly sings vicarious satisfaction, but as rendered in English, while the doctrine is evident, the clarity suffers. Ulrich S. Leupold describes the manifold aspects in which English translations of Luther's hymns suffer much in meter, phrasing, and content.[22]

The work of Christ in atonement kills many birds with one stone and does so in a panoply of ways. Scripture speaks of atonement in words and themes of covenant, testament, sacrifice, Day of Atonement, Passover, Pascal Lamb, redemption, reconciliation, propitiation, justification, the blood of Christ, Lamb of God, payment, Surety, covering, mercy-seat, deliverance, victory over our enemies (the Devil, the world, our sinful selves, death), and ransom, to name some. In Scripture and in dogmatics, these words and themes have usually related and sometimes partially overlapping meanings. Yet each remains a distinct theme. When these are expressed in hymns, owing partly to the poetic and lyrical nature of the hymn texts together with their brevity, sometimes distinct ideas seem to be blended or at least coordinated.

---

[22] Leupold, *op cit.*, 197–201.

For example, ransom and redemption are distinct, but sometimes hymn writers use the word ransom where, from the surrounding context, they seem to have redemption more or equally in mind. For this reason, I have omitted reliance on texts speaking of ransom unless the context clearly joins ransom in blending or coordination with vicarious satisfaction.

The same principle has been followed for other such overlaps, blends, and coordination. An example of a stanza included is "The Royal Banners Forward Go," *ELH* 273, *LSB* 455, *TLH* 168, *LW* 103 and 104, *SBH* 75, *CSB* 91.

> The royal banners forward go
> The cross shows forth redemption's flow,
> Where He in flesh, our flesh
> Our sentence bore, our ransom paid

"Ours sentence bore" plainly is legal, juridical, and forensic and speaks to vicarious satisfaction. The line immediately continues "our ransom paid." The two phrases are glued together. If not a blending of ransom and vicarious satisfaction, it is at least a coordination of them, a singing of distinct but intimately allied themes.

A similar example occurs in "O Jesus So Sweet, O Jesus So Mild," *LSB* 546, *CW1993* 366, *CW 2021* 540.

> O Jesus so sweet, O Jesus so mild
> With God we now are reconciled
> You have for all the ransom paid
> Your Father's righteous anger stayed

"Your Father's righteous anger" plainly is legal, juridical, and forensic. The staying of that anger speaks to propitiation. These are joined in the stanza with the immediately preceding line about ransom. The stanza coordinates ransom with vicarious satisfaction.

The English word "for" has multiple uses. In one use, it is the most succinct way in English to speak of vicarious substitution. "Jesus died for me" easily could be talking about vicarious satisfaction, but the Fordean adversaries employ their high educations, facilities with language, and sophistry to formulate explanations of how "for" has a different meaning. Since this study has, among other things, a polemical purpose to refute the errors of the adversaries, I have usually omitted hymn formulations using only "for" to express substitution. I have done this because I can safely forego reliance on those theoretically ambiguous instances. There is such an abundance of clear evidence without them. But believers of sincere and childlike faith no doubt are hearing and singing those lines in praise to their Substitute who substituted himself into the death they confess they by sin deserved.

Sometimes the lyrics of a hymn express vicarious satisfaction in explicit terms much like prose. Sometimes those expressions are brief, comprised of only a clause or two or four lines. Other times those expressions are extended for two, three, or four stanzas. Sometimes the fact that a stanza expresses vicarious satisfaction is clear only by considering it with the succeeding or preceding stanzas. In such instances, to demonstrate in a writing like this that a hymn is confessing vicarious satisfaction requires presentation of an extended portion of the text.

These properties of the hymns suggest an ordering of the evidence in the following categories:

- Explicit and Brief
- Explicit and Extended
- Implicit

Hymns Reviewed

To fit the work into the time available, I had to limit the hymns to review. A more proper body of hymns to review no doubt could be selected because in the time available, I chose only from among those on hand at home. The sources included are:

AH   *Ambassador Hymnal for Lutheran Worship* (Minneapolis: The Coordinating Committee of the Association of Free Lutheran Congregations, 1994).

CSB   *Common Service Book of the Lutheran Church* (Philadelphia: the Board of Publication of the United Lutheran Church in America, 1917).

CW1993 *Christian Worship* (Milwaukee: Northwestern Publishing House, 1993).

ELH   *Evangelical Lutheran Hymnary* (Mankato, Minnesota: Evangelical Lutheran Synod, 1996).

LSB   *Lutheran Service Book* (St. Louis: Concordia Publishing House, 2006)

LW   *Lutheran Worship* (St. Louis: Concordia Publishing House, 1982)

SBH   *Service Book and Hymnal* (Minneapolis: Augsburg Publishing House and Philadelphia: Lutheran Church in America, 1958).

TLH   *The Lutheran Hymnal* (St. Louis: Concordia Publishing House, 1941)

Because I am a member of the Lutheran Church Missouri Synod familiar with *LSB* and because I had at home a copy of the magnificent *Lutheran Service Book: Companion to the Hymns*, I read all the stanzas of every hymn in *LSB*. Not having time to do that in all the other listed hymnals, I read a subset under the headings of Lent, Holy Week, Good Friday, and Easter. Given that expressions of vicarious satisfaction are spread throughout *LSB* and are not concentrated only under those headings, no doubt I have missed many relevant instances in the non-*LSB* hymnals, which I regret. A person of proper qualifications with adequate time and resources likely would be able to marshal much evidence omitted from this study. If such a person is prompted by this study to carry out the research properly, this study might be considered a success.

Criteria for Identification of Lyrics

Language of Vicarious Satisfaction

The formulation of vicarious satisfaction is set forth under the heading "Formulation of Vicarious Satisfaction" in Chapter One. Criteria for identification of lyrics that confess vicarious satisfaction are derived here from that formulation. That formulation may serve as a foundation for recognizing language that identifies lyrics as confessions of vicarious satisfaction. Some of the elements we could expect to see are:

- God's justice, Law, verdict, judgment, condemnation, and curse
- Active obedience
- Passive obedience
- Substitution
- Imputation, counting, reckoning
- Satisfaction

In the formulation, the element of substitution is seen in "for us" and on "on our behalf." We can recognize language hymn writers use that express substitution. "For us" and "for sinners" frequently are used. But language not expressly used in the above formulation also clearly express the same substitution, such as "in my place" and "in the sinner's stead." These and language of similar import, depending on context, can identify expressions of vicarious satisfaction.

The active obedience of Christ sometimes is expressed by forms of that word, "obedience," "obedient," or "obeying." But hymn writers also refer to his active obedience by its fruits such as "his merit" or "his righteousness." These and language of similar import, depending on context, can identify expressions of vicarious satisfaction.

The passive obedience of Christ often is expressed by words

about his death, such as "death," "dying," "died," and "his Passion." "Christ has humbled himself and become obedient unto death, even the death of the cross." (Philippians 2:8) While death and burial are at the climax of Christ's humiliation, our explanations of the *Small Catechism* teach us five steps in his state of humiliation. Hymn writers tend to associate all the steps with his passive obedience and frequently refer to his lowly birth, life of suffering, crucifixion, death, and burial. They tend to portray all these as forming an organic whole in Christ's mighty work of atonement. That is sound theology. To dissect and dismember any of the steps of Christ's humiliation and exclude it from his passive obedience on our behalf would be rationalistic over-analysis and over-systematization. Language describing Christ's humiliation, depending on context, can identify expression of vicarious satisfaction.

Satisfaction of God for our sin sometimes is expressed directly with words like "satisfied." But hymn writers are not impoverished for poetic expressions of satisfaction. Language showing the response of God to the sacrifice of Christ, depending on context, can identify expression of vicarious satisfaction.

An interesting area is language that speaks all at once to the Law, substitution, and satisfaction. The scripturally related words of counting, reckoning, and imputation are legal words. "Sin is not imputed when there is no law." (Romans 5:13) Language of counting, reckoning, and imputation is used in Bible passages that Lutherans employ as key in teaching justification. In the atonement, our sin was counted, reckoned, and imputed to Christ and the righteousness of Christ was substituted for our sin. Abraham "believed in the LORD, and He accounted it to him for righteousness." (Genesis 15:6, Romans 4:3, James 2:28) Indeed, the whole extended argument Paul makes in Romans 4 and 5 is centered on imputation, reckoning, and counting. In two chapters, relying on the text as rendered in English by the *New King James Version*, Paul explicitly uses terms of imputation six times and terms of counted or accounted six times. It is the backbone of his argument. Remove imputation of Christ's righteousness to us by substitution and the whole epistle to the Romans collapses.

Lutherans teach that we are justified by grace through faith for Christ's sake. That last phrase, "for Christ's sake" is associated with counting, reckoning, and imputation. We are justified when Christ's righteousness and merit are counted to us, reckoned to us, imputed to us. God does not just "up and forgive" as the adversary Forde teaches. He forgives for Christ's sake, which means on account of his vicarious satisfaction for us under the Law.

Lutherans added Public Confession and Absolution to the Service of the Word and the Service of the Sacrament in the Divine Service. The liturgy of "I said, I will confess my transgressions unto the Lord, and You forgave the iniquity of my sin" is from Psalm 32. Should we expect that Lutherans are ignorant of Psalm 32 when we pray this liturgy? Maybe some are, but we should not be. We should know Psalm 32.

> **1** BLESSED *is he whose* transgression *is* forgiven,
> *Whose* sin *is* covered.
> **2** Blessed *is* the man to whom the LORD does not ²impute iniquity,
> And in whose spirit *there is* no deceit.
> **3** When I kept silent, my bones grew old
> Through my groaning all the day long.
> **4** For day and night Your hand was heavy upon me;
> My vitality was turned into the drought of summer.
>   Selah
> **5** I acknowledged my sin to You,
> And my iniquity I have not hidden.
> I said, "I will confess my transgressions to the LORD,"
> And You forgave the iniquity of my sin.   Selah

Note 2 in the above quotation from the *New King James Version* provides an alternative translation for "impute" as "charge his account with." The *English Standard Version* renders it "counts." The *Holman Christian Standard Bible* and the *International Standard Version* use "charge" and "charges." Luther renders it in German in the clause, "*dem der HERR die Missetat nicht zurechnet*," "to whom the LORD does not reckon [alt. charge] transgression."

Thus, not only do Lutherans sing of vicarious satisfaction in our hymns. We begin the Divine Service with allusion to it from the song in Psalm 32.

Hymn writers refer to the legal, forensic, and juridical aspect of Christ's atonement in terms of "the law's demands," "the judgment that stood against me," "just condemnation," and "justice." Despite the objections of the adversaries against Law, justice, and judgment as too uncivilized and barbaric, hymn writers are not ashamed to speak of *avenging* Justice. As rendered in English in "Enslaved by Sin and Bound in Chains," *TLH* 141:4, *CW*1993 102:4, we sing not only of Justice and not only of avenging Justice, but by capitalizing Justice as a proper noun, the hymn translator intimates God Himself as avenging Justice.

> Jesus the Sacrifice became
> To rescue guilty souls from hell
> The spotless, bleeding, dying Lamb
> Beneath avenging Justice fell.

This soundly presents scriptural doctrine, as *Lutheran Service Book: Companion to the Hymns* explains in its commentary on "the deepest stroke . . . that Justice gave" in "Stricken, Smitten, and Afflicted."

> The "deepest stroke," then, was heard in Jesus' cry, "My God, My God, why have You forsaken Me?" (Matthew 27:46) For this was the stroke of *divine* justice, executing judgment for the sins of all humanity. Jesus truly was '*smitten by God*'; yet 'with

His wounds we are healed' (Isaiah 53:4-5).[23]
[emphasis added]

American Lutheran Hymnal even renders it "Was the stroke God's justice gave."[24] "Smitten by God" in Isaiah 53:3 is among the grounds for the lyric "the stroke that Justice gave." Thus, this same intimation where "Enslaved by Sin and Bound in Chains" capitalizes Justice also occurs in the rendering of the phrase in "Stricken, Smitten, and Afflicted" in *TLH* and *ELH*, "But the deepest stroke that pierced Him was the stroke that Justice gave."

This is profoundly dissonant from the claim of adversaries like Paulson who deny that the Law is concordant with and expressive of God's inherent and eternal nature. Hymns like "Salvation unto Us Has Come," *LSB* 555, *AH* 410, *CW1993* 390, *CW2021* 558, *ELH* 227, explicitly confess that the Law must be fulfilled and was fulfilled for us by Christ.

Yet as the Law must be fulfilled
Or we must die despairing,
Christ came and hath God's anger stilled,
Our human nature sharing.
He hath for us the Law obeyed
And thus the Father's vengeance stayed
Which over us impended.

Given the organic and multi-organed fabric of Law-substitution-satisfaction, it will not be surprising to see hymn writers speak of it in a variety of ways. As one more example, consider the language of "curse." Sinners under the Law are cursed because they do not obey it.

For as many as are of the works of the law are under the curse; for it is written, "Cursed is

---

[23] *Companion to the Hymns*, I:311.

[24] *American Lutheran Hymnal* (Columbus, OH: Lutheran Book Concern, 1930) (American Lutheran Church) 399:2.

everyone who does not continue in all things which are written in the book of the law, to do them." (Galatians 3:10, Deuteronomy 27:26)

"What Wondrous Love Is This," *LSB* 543:1, *AH* 72:1, *CW1993* 120:1, *CW2021* 526:1, *ELH* 306:1, a hymn that appears in no less than 241 English hymnals,[25] sings vicarious satisfaction in a most compact line using the language of curse, "To bear the dreadful curse for my soul." This confesses that my soul was under the curse of the Law for disobeying it. It confesses that Jesus bore my curse "for my soul." There is no escaping substitution, vicarious satisfaction, and Law in this lyric.

Foci of Criteria Recapped

We can recap the foregoing as follows:

- Satisfaction language
- Substitution language, including language of "wonderful exchange"
- Active obedience language
- Passive obedience language
- Legal language

The mere presence of such language, which alerts us to take a closer look at the passage, is not adequate alone to conclude that a hymn writer is speaking of vicarious satisfaction. The context and usage of the language always remain indispensable to the criteria for identifying vicarious satisfaction in the hymns.

Criteria Illustrated by Examples

Let us apprehend the criteria by way of examples and illustrations.

---

[25] *Hymnary,com*, https://hymnary.org/search?qu=what+wondrous+love.

A common phrase in Lutheran hymns is "Jesus' blood and merit."

The usage of the word "merit" in this common phrase often references the full righteousness of Christ in his active obedience, and hence speaks to vicarious satisfaction. In Luther's "wonderful exchange," Christ exchanges our sin and his righteous merit. That is vicarious satisfaction.

The usage of the word "blood" typically references Christ's death on the cross. "The wages of sin is death." (Romans 6:23) By humbling himself to death on the cross where his blood was shed for the remission of sin, Jesus suffered the penalty of the Law for us. This passive obedience that atones for us is vicarious satisfaction.

The hymn "Through Jesus' Blood and Merit," LSB 746, CW1993 445, ELH 414, LW 369, TLH 372 confesses:

> Through Jesus' blood and merit
> I am at peace with God

Paul says that in our sinfulness, we are "enmity" against God (Romans 8:7). Therefore, on our own we have no peace with him. This hymn confesses what reversed that calamity. Through Jesus' blood and merit, the enmity is gone and peace reigns. (Romans 5:1, 14:17, 15:13)

Thomas Kingo's cherished Baptism hymn, "He That Believes and is Baptized," SBH 259, AH 270, ELH 241, CW1993 299, CW2021 692, LW 225, TLH 301, LSB 601 ties salvation, Baptism, and eternal life to God looking on us "through Jesus' Blood and merit."

"Like the Golden Sun Ascending," TLH 207, CW1993 147, CW2021 470, ELH 354 may be used as an example of context clarifying that usage of the English word "for" speaks of vicarious substitution.

> Thou hast died for my transgression
> All my sins on Thee were laid
> Thou hast won for me salvation

On the cross my debt was paid

The adversaries might try to manipulate the first line to make "for" means something besides Christ being substituted in our place. But the next line elucidates what "for" means. "All my sins on Thee were laid." They are my sins, but they are laid on him. That is substitution. Then the next line says that by being substituted into my sins and dying for my transgression, "Thou has won for me salvation." How has He done that. To childlike believers, that answer is obvious, but the stanza goes on to make it explicit, saying, "On the cross my debt was paid." Sin makes us debtors to God. When Jesus pays our debt for us, that is substitution and satisfaction. Put all that together and you have vicarious satisfaction.

Hymns like "To Jordan's River Came Our Lord," *LSB* 405, *CW1993* 89, *CW2021* 377 explicitly say that Jesus acted as "our substitute" even in actions like being baptized by John. John's was a baptism of repentance. Jesus had no sin of his own for which to repent. John, therefore, tried to prevent Jesus' from being baptized. But Jesus told him to allow it "to fulfill all righteousness." (Matthew 3:15). Jesus already was fully righteous, so for whom was He fulfilling all righteousness? He did this for us, to give us his righteousness.

> Luther captured the primary meaning of his Baptism: "[Christ] accepted it from John for the reason that he was entering into our stead, indeed, our person, that is, becoming a sinner for us, taking upon himself the sins which he had not committed, and wiping them out and drowning them in his holy baptism (*AE* 51:315)[26]

---

[26] *The Lutheran Study Bible* (St. Louis: Concordia Publishing House, 2009), 1582 n. 3:15. The citation to *AE* is to Martin Luther, *Luther's Works: American Edition* (St. Louis: Concordia Publishing Houses; Philadelphia:; Muhlenberg

"Entering into our stead" is plain language of substitution. Thus, "To Jordan's River Came Our Lord" continues, explicitly using the language "Christ, our substitute."

> The Savior came to be baptized
> The Son of God in flesh disguised
> To stand beneath the Father's will
> And all His righteousness fulfill
> Now rise, faint hearts, be resolute
> This man is Christ, our substitute
> He was baptized in Jordan's stream
> Proclaimed Redeemer, Lord supreme

Whole stanzas of favorite hymns make no sense without substitution. Consider this stanza from "Stricken, Smitten, and Afflicted," *LSB* 451, *TLH* 153, *ELH* 297, *CW1993* 127, *LW* 116, *AH* 75, ALH 399.[27]

> Ye who think of sin but lightly
> Nor suppose the evil great
> Here may view its nature rightly
> Here its guilt may estimate
> Mark the Sacrifice appointed
> See Who bears the awful load
> 'Tis the Word, the Lord's Anointed
> Son of Man, and Son of God

How may we "here," that is, at the cross, views the nature of sin rightly? How may we estimate its guilt? We may do so by marking the Sacrifice appointed, by seeing Who bears the awful load. If He is not bearing our sin, if He is not our substitute, if He is not making vicarious satisfaction, then our sin, its nature, and its guilt are not seen at the cross. It is just because of vicarious satisfaction that the cross exposes the enormity of sin by showing Who had to be our Substitute.

Press; and Philadelphia: Fortress Press).

[27] *American Lutheran Hymnal* (Columbus, OH: Lutheran Book Concern, 1930) (American Lutheran Church).

"When You Woke That Thursday Morning," *LSB* 445, *CW1996* 717, *CW2021* 416 confesses the same thing in a similar but varied formulation.

> When but One could pay sin's wages
> You assumed their dreadful sum

From this we see that language of debt and payment can speak to vicarious satisfaction. Similarly, the beloved Baptism hymn, "God's Own Child, I Gladly Say It," *LSB* 594, *ELH* 246, *CW2021* 679 confesses:

> God's own child, I gladly say it: I am baptized into Christ
> He, because I could not pay it, gave my full redemption
>   price
> Do I need earth's treasures many? I have one worth more
>   than any
> That brought me salvation free, Lasting to eternity

This hymn uses the language of payment and expresses the payment of "redemption price." The word redemption is drawn from the law of debt and mortgages. When a debtor defaults in making payments, the creditor may judicially foreclose the mortgage and take the land. Moses' law gave debtors a right of redemption if they later could muster payment of the debt. That law also allowed vicars (substitutes) closely related to a debtor to pay the redemption price on their behalf. If no qualified person could redeem, then God himself redeemed all bonded land in the Jubilee Year. (Leviticus 25:23-38) In the hymn, "He, because I could not pay it, gave my full redemption price" Christ as our qualified Vicar makes vicarious satisfaction. He is qualified because, in the incarnation, He is fully human, our Brother.

The expressions in the third line about one treasure worth more than any refers to the treasury of Christ's righteous merits. The hymn gives us words to confess and teach one another that in Baptism, Christ gives us his treasure of righteousness. The last line plainly says his giving that treasure brought me eternal salvation. That is vicarious satisfaction.

Lutheran hymns expose the errors of the Fordean adversaries as being completely untenable. In the broadly used hymn, "The Death of Jesus Christ, Our Lord," *LSB* 634:2, *TLH* 163:2, *ELH* 329:2, *CW1993* 135:2, *CW2021* 677:2, *LW* 107:2, *THOS* 234:2[28], consider how the rejection of "the legal scheme" by Paulson and company fares against what the church confesses:

> He blotted out with His own blood
> The judgment that against us stood
> For us He full atonement made,
> And all our debt He fully paid.

Face it. The word "judgment" is forensic, juridical, and legal. These lyrics are strongly referent to Colossians 2:14 (ESV): "Having forgiven us all our trespasses, by canceling the record of debt that stood against us with its legal demands. This he set aside, nailing it to the cross."[29] *The Lutheran Study*

---

[28] *The Hymnal and Order of Service* (Rock Island, IL: Augustana Book Concern, 1926) (Evangelical Augustana Lutheran Synod of North America).

[29] NKJV: "Having wiped out the handwriting of [NKJV note 9, alt. "certificate of with its] requirements that was against us, which was contrary to us. And He has taken it out of the way, having nailed it to the cross."

NASB: "Having canceled the certificate of debt consisting of decrees against us, which was hostile to us; and He has taken it out of the way, having nailed it to the cross.

NIV: "Having canceled the charge of our legal indebtedness, which stood against us and condemned us; he has taken it away, nailing it to the cross."

HCSB: "He erased the certificate of debt, with its obligations, that was against us and opposed to us, and has taken it out of the way by nailing it to the cross."

ISV: "Having erased the charges that were brought against us, along with their obligations that were hostile to us. He took those charges away when he nailed them to the cross."

LEB: "Having destroyed the certificate of indebtedness in ordinances against us, which was hostile to us, and removed it out of the way by nailing it to the cross."

NET: "He has destroyed what was against us, a certificate of indebtedness

Bible note on this verse says,

> 2:14 *record . . . legal demands*. The debtor kept a
> handwritten bill of indebtedness; in this case, it is
> the record of all our violations of God's Law. This
> record is wiped away by Jesus' death on the cross.[30]

The work of Christ on the cross was not merely to make a
grand gesture of a free-floating general amnesty that results
in atonement only if and when someone believes a bloodless
word of absolution. No. Christ atoned there and then on the
cross. Christ blotted out the judgment with his own blood. He
cancelled the record of debt. He nailed that record to the
cross, showing that it was exhausted and fulfilled in his
death. My faith is not what blots out the judgment. Christ's
blood blots it out. Faith does not cause justification but
merely receives it. As we sing in "Let Me Be Thine Forever,"
LSB 689, *CW1996* 596, *CW2021* 715, *ELH* 427, *LW* 257, *SBH* 506,
TLH 334, *CSB* 271:

> For Thou has dearly bought me
> With blood and bitter pain
> Grant that in Jesus' merit
> I always may confide

When we confess that we are saved by faith, that does not
mean we confide in our faith. We confide in Christ, his blood,
his bitter pain, and his merit.

Returning to "The Death of Jesus Christ, Our Lord," in
addition to judgment being forensic, debt is legal and
foreclosure is juridical and forensic. Those last two lines
literally say that Christ's atonement was a payment of our
debt.

---

expressed in decrees opposed to us. He has taken it away by nailing it to the
cross."

[30] *The Lutheran Study Bible* (St. Louis: Concordia Publishing House, 2009),
2046, n. 2:14.

The stanza accords with Paul in Galatians 4:4: "When the fullness of the time had come, God sent forth His Son, born of a woman, born under the law, to redeem those who were under the law, that we might receive the adoption as sons." Even adoption is not by nature but by law.[31] Rid that Scripture of "the legal scheme" and there would be no redemption, no adoption, no justification – no Christianity.

In the realm of bluntness, the church sings in "I am Content! My Jesus Ever Lives," LSB 468:1, TLH 196:1, CW1993 158:1, CW2021 464:1,

> He has fulfilled the Law of God for me
> God's wrath He has appeased

How can anyone evade "the legal scheme" of "He has fulfilled the Law of God for me?" How can anyone evade the substitution of Christ fulling the Law for me? How can anyone evade the satisfaction of God's wrath being appeased? How can anyone sustain the claim that God, before and without the sacrifice of Christ, just "up and forgave" sin when we sing that what appeased God's wrath was Christ's living and dying for us?

Similarly, how can one evade substitution under the Law and vicarious substitution in "The Night Will Soon Be Ending," LSB 337:2?

> Thus God, the judge offended
> Bears all our sins deserve

If "the judge offended" is not legal, juridical, and forensic, what would be? If God "bears all our sins deserve" is not substitutionary, what would be?

---

[31] Admittedly, it is taken over by the Gospel in Baptism. Moses, whose name means "drawn from water," was drawn from water in an ark. The ark of Noah and the ark of Moses both prefigure Baptism. When Moses was draw from water in this foreshadowing of Baptism, he was adopted. We, too, are adopted as sons of God in our Baptisms by Gospel grace. In both Law and Gospel, however, sonship by adoption is not by nature.

In the same way, and without any necessity of elucidating it by analysis or commentary, "Lift Up Your Heads You Everlasting Doors," *LSB* 339:3 plainly sings the righteousness of Christ meeting the Law's demands in claiming the cross as his throne.

> Who may ascend Mount Zion's holy hill
> To do God's will
> The One whose unstained hands
> Can meet the Law's demands
> Whose purity within
> Reveals One free from sin
> Come praise this King who claims the cross as throne
> Praise Him alone

A hymn that tightly wraps together many elements of vicarious satisfaction in four lines is "Before the Throne of God Above," *LSB* 574, *CW2021* 561.

> Because the sinless Savior died
> My sinful soul is counted free
> For God, the Just, is satisfied
> To look on Him and pardon me

The active obedience of Christ: "the sinless Savior." The passive obedience of Christ: "Savior died." Imputation: "my sinful soul is counted free." The Law and justice: "For God, the Just." Satisfaction: "is satisfied." Substitution: "to look on Him and pardon me."

For a final example of an explicit and brief confession of vicarious satisfaction, consider "Of My Life the Life," *ELH* 336.[32]

> For my proud and haughty spirit
> Thy humiliation paid
> For my death Thy death and merit

---

[32] Also in *The Lutheran Hymnary* (Minneapolis: Augsburg Publishing House, 1913), 319:4.

> Have a full atonement made

My proud and haughty spirit references sin. "Thy humiliation" references Christ humbling himself to the death of the cross. "For my death Thy death and merit" is a plain and compact confession of the active obedience of Christ in "merit," of the passive obedience of Christ in "death," and substitution in "For my death Thy death." All these come to satisfaction in "Have full atonement made."

As an example of the importance of context, consider "Make Songs of Joy," *LSB* 484:2, *LW* 132:2.

> Our life was purchased by His loss
> He died our death upon the cross

The language of purchase by itself is ambiguous. It could refer to ransom, which in and of itself would not be vicarious satisfaction. It could refer to redemption and thus could involve vicarious satisfaction, though not necessarily. But the lyric, "He died our death" plainly states substitution and passive obedience for us under the Law. Taken together, then, this hymn sings vicarious satisfaction.

Let us review just two instances of explicit and *extended* expressions of vicarious satisfaction. The first is one of Paul Gerhardt's many great hymns, "A Lamb Goes Uncomplaining Forth," *LSB* 438, *TLH* 142, *ELH* 331, *CW1996* 100, *CW2021* 422. "Except for Gerhardt's other Passion hymn, 'O sacred Head, now wounded' (*LSB* 449-50), it is probably the most significant Good Friday text in Lutheran practice."[33] *LSB* uses stanzas 1–3 and 10 of the original.[34] Here we review stanzas 1, 2 and 4 from *LSB*.

> 1. A Lamb goes uncomplaining forth,

---

[33] *Lutheran Service Book: Companion to the Hymns*, (St. Louis: Concordia Publishing House, 2019), I.277.

[34] *Companion to the Hymns*, I:278.

The guilt of sinners bearing
And, laden with the sins of earth,
None else the burden sharing;
Goes patient on, grows weak and faint,
To slaughter led without complaint,
That spotless life to offer,
He bears the stripes, the wounds, the lies,
The mockery, and yet replies,
"All this I gladly suffer."

2. This Lamb is Christ, the soul's great friend,
The Lamb of God, our Savior,
Whom God the Father chose to send
To gain for us His favor.
"Go forth, My Son," the Father said,
"And free My children from their dread
Of guilt and condemnation.
The wrath and stripes are hard to bear,
But by Your passion they will share
The fruit of Your salvation."

4. Lord, when Your glory I shall see
And taste Your kingdom's pleasure,
Your blood my royal robe shall be,
My joy beyond all measure!
When I appear before Your throne,
Your righteousness shall be my crown;
With these I need not hide me.
And there, in garments richly wrought,
As Your own bride shall we be brought
To stand in joy beside You.

The single word "Lamb" in the opening phrase would refer to what, if not "the Lamb of God who takes away the sin of the world?" (John 1:29) Verse two rounds out the reference to "the Lamb of God, our Savior." How, in the Bible, does a lamb take away sin and save? He does it in the same way that the next two lines of the stanza say, "The guilt of sinners bearing, and, laden with the sins of earth." The Lamb of God bears our sin and substitutes for us in what we are about to sing next. He goes on to slaughter without complaint. Plainly, this references the death of Christ.

The sixth line, "That spotless life to offer" plainly references the active obedience of Christ. No one else has succeeded in living a life without spot. Though with extreme brevity, the word "offer," in the contexts of both the hymn and Scripture, intimates both a satisfying sacrifice and a substitution of the Lamb for sinners. Without both satisfaction and substitution, the Lamb could not obtain the Father's favor as confessed in the fourth line of stanza 2.

In the second half of the second stanza, the passion, which is to say, the death of the Lamb, frees sinners of guilt, condemnation, wrath, and stripes, and gives them salvation. This is an extended depiction of satisfaction and its effects.

For the sake of time and to avoid being pedestrian, let us skip forward to the last stanza. "Your righteousness shall be my crown," references the active obedience of Christ for us in his fulfillment of all righteousness. That we are allowed to wear Christ's righteousness as our crown is a gleaming depiction of wonderful exchange and substitution. In Christ's state of exaltation, his mighty work of vicarious satisfaction is on parade.

"Your blood my royal robe shall be" says that the blood and death of Christ cover my sins and make me royal. When they had fallen into sin, Adam and Eve tried to hide themselves from the presence of the Lord (Genesis 3:8), but now with the crown of Christ's righteousness and the royal robes of Christ's blood, we sing, "With these I need not hide me." We wear the active and passive obedience of Christ as our own. This is a pageantry of vicarious satisfaction.

A hymn that wraps together many elements of vicarious satisfaction is "O Perfect Life of Love," *LSB* 452, *TLH* 170, *CW1993* 138, *CW2021* 431, *CSB* 103, *SBH* 89.

    O perfect life of love

All, all, is finished now
all that he left his throne above
to do for us below

No work is left undone
of all the Father willed
his toil, his sorrows, one by one
the Scriptures have fulfilled

And on his thorn-crowned head
and on his sinless soul
our sins in all their guilt were laid
that He might make us whole

In perfect love he dies
for me he dies, for me
O all-atoning Sacrifice
you died to make me free

In ev'ry time of need
before the judgment throne
your works, O Lamb of God, I'll plead
your merits, not my own

Hymns Singing Vicarious Satisfaction

Following is a presentation of some of the evidence discovered by the described review of the defined body of hymns.

Selected for presentation are:

- Explicit and brief excerpts from 58 hymns
- Explicit and extended excerpts from 35 hymns
- Implicit excerpts from 5 hymns

Explicit and Brief

This category includes expressions of vicarious satisfaction that are explicit and relatively brief. In the quotations below, often only relevant portions of stanzas are rendered to retain focus and reduce the length of this writing.

Through Jesus' Blood and Merit, LSB 746, CW 1993 445, ELH 414, LW 369, TLH 372

> Through Jesus' blood and merit
> I am at peace with God

Like the Golden Sun Ascending, TLH 207 CW1993 147, CW2021 470, ELH 354

> Thou hast died for my transgression
> All my sins on Thee were laid
> Thou hast won for me salvation
> On the cross my debt was paid

Sweet the Moments, Rich in Blessing, TLH 155, ELH 300

> Here we rest in wonder viewing
> All our sins on Jesus laid
> Here we see redemption flowing
> From the sacrifice He made
>
> Here we find the dawn of heaven
> While upon the cross we gaze
> See our trespasses forgiven
> And our songs of triumph raise

He Was Wounded for Our Transgressions, AH 77

> He was wounded for our transgressions
> He bore our sin in His body on the tree
> He was numbered among transgressors
> We did esteem Him forsaken by His God
> As our sacrifice He died
> That the law be satisfied
> And all our sin, and all our sin
> And all our sin was laid on Him

Here, O My Lord, I See Thee Face to Face, LSB 631

> Mine is the sin, but Thine the righteousness
> Mine is the guilt, but Thine the cleansing blood
> Here is my robe, my refuge, and my peace
> Thy blood, Thy righteousness, O Lord my God

The Death of Jesus Christ, Our Lord, LSB 634, TLH 163, ELH 329,
CW1993 135, CW2021 677, LW 107, THOS 234[35]

> He blotted out with His own blood
> The judgment that against us stood
> For us He full atonement made,
> And all our debt He fully paid.

Thanks to Thee, O Christ, Victorious, LSB 548

> Thou hast dies for my transgression
> All my sins on Thee were laid
> Thou hast won for me salvation
> On the cross my debt was paid

I am Content! My Jesus Ever Lives, LSB 468, TLH 196, CW1993 158,
CW2021 464

> He has fulfilled the Law of God for me
> God's wrath He has appeased

Make Songs of Joy, LSB 484

> Our life was purchased by His loss
> He died our death upon the cross

Christ the Lord Is Risen Today, LSB 463, SBH 99, AH 104, TLH 190

> For the sheep the Lamb has bled
> Sinless in the sinner's stead

The Night Will Soon Be Ending, LSB 337

> Thus God, the judge offended
> Bears all our sins deserve
> The guilty need not cower
> For God has reconciled

Lift Up Your Heads You Everlasting Doors, LSB 339

> Who may ascend Mount Zion's holy hill
> To do God's will

---

[35] *The Hymnal and Order of Service* (Rock Island, IL: Augustana Book Concern, 1926) (Evangelical Augustana Lutheran Synod of North America).

The One whose unstained hands
Can meet the Law's demands
Whose purity within
Reveals One free from sin
Come praise this King who claims the cross as throne
Praise Him alone

When All the World Was Cursed, LSB 346

Behold the Lamb of God
That bears the world's transgression
Whose sacrifice removes
The devil's dread oppression
Behold the Lamb of God
Who takes away our sin
Who for our peace and joy
Will full atonement win

God Loves Me Dearly, LSB 392

Jesus, my Savior
Himself did offer
Jesus, my Savior
Paid all I owe

Lamb of God, Pure and Holy, LSB 434

Lamb of God, pure and holy
Who on the cross didst suffer
Ever patient and lowly
Thyself to scorn didst offer
All sins Thou borest for us
Else had despair reigned o'er us

When You Woke That Thursday Morning, LSB 445, CW1996 717, CW2021 416

When You woke that Thursday morning
Savior, teacher, faithful friend
Thoughts of self and safety scorning
Knowing how the day would end
Lamb of God, foretold for ages
Now at last the hour had come
When but One could pay sin's wages

You assumed their dreadful sum

Jesus, In Your Dying Woes, LSB 447

> Jesus, all our ransom paid
> All Your Father's will obeyed
> By Your suff'rings perfect made
> Hear us, holy Jesus

O Day Full of Grace, LSB 503

> For Christ bore our sins, and not His own
> When He on the cross was hanging

O, for a Thousand Tongues to Sing, LSB 528

> See all your sins on Jesus laid
> The Lamb of God was slain
> His soul was once an off'ring made
> Four ev'ry soul of man

When I Behold Jesus Christ, LSB 542

> You had no sin, holy Lord
> But You were tortured, tried
> On Golgotha there for all
> My sins You bled and died

O Christ, Our Hope, Our Hearts' Desire, LSB 553

> How vast Your mercy to accept
> The burden of our sin
> And bow Your head in cruel death
> To make us clean within

God's Own Child, I Gladly Say it, LSB 594, ELH 246, CW2021 679

> God's own child, I gladly say it: I am baptized into
> Christ!
> He, because I could not pay it, gave my full redemption
> price.
> Do I need earth's treasures many? I have one worth
> more than any
> That brought me salvation free, Lasting to eternity!

Jesus Christ, Our Blessed Savior, LSB 627, ELH 316

> Jesus Christ, our blessed Savior
> Turned away God's wrath forever
> By His bitter grief and woe
> He saved us from the evil foe

The We Adore, O Hidden Savior, LSB 640

> Thy blood, O Lord, one drop has pow'r to win
> Forgiveness for our world and all its sin

Saints, See the Cloud of Witnesses, LSB 667

> Come, let us fix our sight on Christ who suffered
> He faced the cross, His sinless life He offered
> He scorned the shame, He died, our death enduring
> Our hope securing

Let Me Be Thine Forever, LSB 689, CW1996 596, CW 2021 715, ELH 427, LW 257, SBH 506, TLH 334, CSB 271

> For Thou has dearly bought me
> With blood and bitter pain
> Grant that in Jesus' merit
> I always may confide

O Holy Spirit, Grant Us Grace, LSB 693

> The hour of death cannot bring loss
> When we are sheltered by the cross
> That cancelled our transgression

I Am Trusting Thee, Lord Jesus, LSB 729

> I am trusting Thee for cleansing
> In the crimson flood
> Trusting Thee to make me holy
> By Thy blood

When Peace, like a River, LSB 763

> He lives – oh, the bliss of this glorious thought
> My sin, not in part, but the whole
> Is nailed to His cross and I bear it no more
> Praise the Lord, praise the Lord, O my soul

Alabaré, LSB 799

> Worthy is Christ the Lamb who was slain
> Whose blood has set us free from every sin

How Great Thou Art, LSB 801

> But when I think that God, His Son not sparing
> Sent Him to die, I scarce can take it in
> That on the cross my burden gladly bearing
> He bled and died to take away my sin

Spread the Reign of God the Lord, LSB 830

> Tell of our Redeemer's grace
> Who to save our human race
> And to pay rebellion's price
> Gave Himself as sacrifice

Praise the One Who Breaks the Darkness, LSB 849

> Let us praise the Word Incarnate
> Christ, who suffered in our place
> Jesus died and rose victorious
> That we may know God by grace

Gracious Savior, Grant Your Blessing, LSB 860

> Make their love a living picture
> Showing how You loved Your bride
> When You gave Yourself to cleanse her
> When for her You bled and died
> Jesus, You have made her holy
> Pure and fair her radiant train
> To Yourself, Your Church presenting
> Without wrinkle, spot, or stain

Wide Open Are Thy Hands, SBH 66, CSB 65, ELH 265

> Wide open are thy hands
> Paying with more than gold
> The awful debt of guilty men
> Forever and of old
> Jesus, clad in purple raiment
> For man's evils making payment

At the cross, her station keeping, SBH 84

> For his people's sins chastised
> She beheld her son despised

O darkest woe, SBH 87, TLH 167, ELH 332

> O sorrow dread
> Our God is dead
> He paid our great redemption
> Jesus' death upon the cross
> Gained for us salvation
>
> O sinful man
> It was the ban
> Of death on thee that brought him
> Down to suffer for thy sins
> And such woe that wrought him
>
> Behold thy Lord
> The Lamb of God
> Blood-sprinkled lies before thee
> Pour out his life that he
> May to life restore thee

Christ Jesus lay in death's strong bands, SBH 98, AH 114

> Christ Jesus lay in death's strong bands
> For our offenses given
> But now at God's right hand he stands
> And brings us life from heaven

What Wondrous Love Is This, LSB 543, AH 72, CW1993 120, CW2021 526, ELH 306

> What wondrous love is this
> That caused the Lord of bliss
> To bear the dreadful curse for my soul
> When I was sinking down
> Beneath God's righteous frown
> Christ laid aside His crown for my soul

The Hour in Dark Gethsemane, AH 76

> When I among the solemn trees
> In spirit gazed around
> I saw the burden of my sin
> On Him with judgment bound

Jesus, Name All Names Above, AH 8

> Jesus, clad in purple raiment
> For man's evils making payment

When Our Heads Are Bowed with Woe, CSB 76, ELH 274

> Thou the shame, the grief, hast known
> Though the sins were not Thine own
> Thou hast deigned their load to bear
> Jesus, Son of Mary, hear

Enslaved by Sin and Bound in Chains, TLH 141, CW1993 102

> Jesus the Sacrifice became
> To rescue guilty souls from hell
> The spotless, bleeding, dying Lamb
> Beneath avenging Justice fell.

Jesus Christ, Our Lord Most Holy, TLH 169, ELH 285

> Jesus Christ, our Lord most holy
> Lamb of God so pure and lowly
> Blameless, blameless, on the cross art offered
> Sinless, sinless, for our sins has suffered

Lord Jesus, We Give Thanks To Thee, TLH 173

> Lord Jesus, we give thanks to Thee
> That Thou hast died to set us free
> Made righteous thro' Thy precious blood
> We now are reconciled to God

Draw Nigh and Take the Body of the Lord, ELH 314

> Victims were offered by the law of old
> Which in a type this heav'nly myst'ry hold

Of My Life the Life, ELH 336[36]

> For my proud and haughty spirit
> Thy humiliation paid
> For my death Thy death and merit
> Have a full atonement made

Come, Thou Long-Expected Jesus, LSB 338

> By Thine all-sufficient merit
> Raise us to Thy glorious throne

O Sing of Christ, LSB 362

> What Adam lost, none could reclaim
> And Paradise was barred
> Until the second Adam came
> To mend what sin had marred
> For when the time was full and right
> God sent His only son
> He came to us as life and light
> And our redemption won

Jesus, Once with Sinners Numbered, LSB 404

> Jesus, once with sinners numbered
> Full obedience was Your path
> You, by death, have consecrated
> Water in this saving bath

To Jordan's River Came Our Lord, LSB 405, CW1993 89, CW2021 377

> The Savior came to be baptized
> The Son of God in flesh disguised
> To stand beneath the Father's will
> And all His righteousness fulfill
>
> Now rise, faint hearts, be resolute
> This man is Christ, our substitute
> He was baptized in Jordan's stream

---

[36] Also in *The Lutheran Hymnary* (Minneapolis: Augsburg Publishing House, 1913), 319.

Proclaimed Redeemer, Lord supreme

We Sing the Praise of Him Who Died, LSB 429, CSB 66, TLH 178

Inscribed upon the cross we see
In shining letters "God is love"
He bears our sins upon the tree
He brings us mercy from above

To Christ, who won for sinners grace
By bitter grief and anguish sore
Be praise from all the ransomed race
Forever and forevermore

Glory Be to Jesus, LSB 433, SBH 76, TLH 158, ELH 283

Blest through endless ages
Be the precious stream
Which from endless torment
Did the world redeem

Abel's blood for vengeance
Pleaded to the skies
But the blood of Jesus
For our pardon cries.

*The Royal Banners Forward Go, ELH 273, LSB 455, TLH 168, LW 103
and 104, SBH 75, CSB 91*

The royal banners forward go
The cross shows forth redemption's flow
Where He in flesh, our flesh
Our sentence bore, our ransom paid

Where deep for us the spear was dyed
Life's torrent rushing from His side
To wash us in that precious flood
Where flowed the water and the blood

O Jesus So Sweet, O Jesus So Mild, LSB 546, CW1993 366, CW 2021 540

O Jesus so sweet, O Jesus so mild
With God we now are reconciled
You have for all the ransom paid

Your Father's righteous anger stayed

Behold a Host, Arrayed in White, LSB 676

These are the saints of glorious fame
Whom from the great affliction came
And in the flood
Of Jesus blood
Are cleansed from guilt and shame

The Kingdom Satan Founded, ELH 259

To God I raise my crying
Before the mercy-seat
And on His Word relying
I grace of Him entreat
That He for Jesus' sake
Would cleanse my soul and spirit
Through Jesus' blood and merit
And Satan's power break

We Bless Thee, Jesus Christ Our Lord, ELH 275

We bless Thee, Jesus Christ our Lord
Forever be Thy name adored
For Thou, the sinless One hast died
That sinners might be justified

O very Man, and very God
Who hast redeemed us with Thy blood
From death eternal set us free
And make us one with God in Thee

Explicit and Extended

This category includes expressions of vicarious satisfaction that are explicit and more extended. In the quotations below, sometimes only relevant portions of stanzas are rendered to retain focus and reduce the length of this writing.

Upon the Cross Extended, LSB 453, TLH 171, ELH 304

Who is it, Lord, that bruised you
Who has so sore abused you

and caused you all your woe
We all must make confession
of sin and dire transgression
while you no ways of evil know

I caused your grief and sighing
by evils multiplying
as countless as the sands
I caused the woes unnumbered
with which your soul is cumbered
your sorrows raised by wicked hands

[TLH:5, ELH:5] 'Tis I who should be smitten
My doom should here be written
Bound hand foot in hell
The fetters and the scourging
The floods around Thee surging
'Tis I who have deserved them

[TLH:6, ELH:6] The load Thou takest on Thee
That pressed so sorely on me
It crushed me to the ground
The cross for me enduring
The crown for me securing
My healing in Thy wounds is found

[ELH:7] A crown of thorns Thou wearest
My shame and score Thou bearest
That I might ransomed be
My Bondsman, ever willing
My place with patience filling
From sin and guilt has made me free

Your soul in griefs unbounded,
your head with thorns surrounded
you died to ransom me
The cross for me enduring
the crown for me securing
you healed my wounds and set me free

[TLH:10, ELH:10] How God at our transgression
To anger gives expression
How loud His thunders role
How fearfully He smiteth
How sorely He requiteth
All this Thy sufferings teach my soul

A Lamb Goes Uncomplaining Forth, LSB 438, TLH 142, ELH 331,
CW1996 100, CW2021 422

A Lamb goes uncomplaining forth
The guilt of sinners bearing
And, laden with the sins of earth
None else the burden sharing
Goes patient on, grows weak and faint
To slaughter led without complaint
That spotless life to offer
He bears the stripes, the wounds, the lies
The mockery, and yet replies
"All this I gladly suffer"

This Lamb is Christ, the soul's great friend
The Lamb of God, our Savior
Whom God the Father chose to send
To gain for us His favor
"Go forth, My Son," the Father said
"And free My children from their dread
Of guilt and condemnation
The wrath and stripes are hard to bear
But by Your passion they will share
The fruit of Your salvation"

"Yes, Father, yes, most willingly
I'll bear what You command Me
My will conforms to Your decree
I'll do what You have asked Me"
O wondrous Love, what have You done
The Father offers up His Son
Desiring our salvation

O Love, how strong You are to save
You lay the One into the grave
Who built the earth's foundation

Lord, when Your glory I shall see
And taste Your kingdom's pleasure
Your blood my royal robe shall be
My joy beyond all measure
When I appear before Your throne
Your righteousness shall be my crown
With these I need not hide me
And there, in garments richly wrought
As Your own bride shall we be brought
To stand in joy beside You

O Dearest Jesus, What Law Hast Thou Broken, LSB 439, TLH 143, ELH 292

Whence come these sorrows, whence this mortal anguish
It is my sins for which Thou, Lord, must languish
Yea, all the wrath, the woe, Thou dost inherit
This I do merit.

What punishment so strange is suffered yonder
The Shepherd dies for sheep that loved to wander
The Master pays the debt His servants owe Him
Who would not know Him

The sinless Son of God must die in sadness
The sinful child of man may live in gladness
Man forfeited his life and is acquitted
God is committed

O Sacred Head, Now Wounded, LSB 449, CSB 99, TLH 172, ELH 334

[TLH v 4] My burden in Thy Passion
Lord, Thou has borne for me
For it was my transgression
Which bro't this woe on Thee
I cast me down before Thee
Wrath were my rightful lot

Have Mercy, I implore Thee
Redeemer, spurn me not

What thou, my Lord, hast suffered
was all for sinners' gain
Mine, mine was the transgression
but thine the deadly pain
Lo, here I fall, my Savior
'Tis I deserve Thy place
Look on me with thy favor
and grant to me thy grace

*Stricken, Smitten, and Afflicted, LSB 451, TLH 153, ELH 297, CW1993
127, LW 116, AH 75, ALH 399*

Tell me, ye who hear Him groaning
Was there ever grief like His
Friends through fear His cause disowning
Foes insulting His distress
Many hands were raised to wound Him
None would interpose to save
But the deepest stroke that pierced Him
Was the stroke that Justice gave

Ye who think of sin but lightly
Nor suppose the evil great
Here may view its nature rightly
Here its guilt may estimate
Mark the Sacrifice appointed
See Who bears the awful load
'Tis the Word, the Lord's Anointed
Son of Man, and Son of God

Here we have a firm foundation
Here the refuge of the lost
Christ the Rock of our salvation
His the Name of which we boast
Lamb of God for sinners wounded
Sacrifice to cancel guilt
None shall ever be confounded

Who on Him their hope have built

O Perfect Life of Love, LSB 452, TLH 170, CW1993 138, CW2021 431,
CSB 103, SBH 89

O perfect life of love
All, all, is finished now
all that he left his throne above
to do for us below

No work is left undone
of all the Father willed
his toil, his sorrows, one by one
the Scriptures have fulfilled

And on his thorn-crowned head
and on his sinless soul
our sins in all their guilt were laid
that He might make us whole

In perfect love he dies
for me he dies, for me
O all-atoning Sacrifice
you died to make me free

In ev'ry time of need
before the judgment throne
your works, O Lamb of God, I'll plead
your merits, not my own

Christ, the Life of All the Living, LSB 420, TLH 151, ELH 333

Thou, Ah Thou has taken on Thee
Bonds and stripes, a cruel rod
Pain and scorn were heaped upon Thee
O Thou sinless Son of God
Thus didst Thou my soul deliver
From the bonds of sin forever

Thou hast born the smiting only
That my wounds might all be whole

Thou has suffered, sad and lonely
Rest to give my weary soul
Yea, the curse of God enduring
Blessing unto me securing

Thou hast suffered great affliction
And has borne it patiently
Even death by crucifixion
Fully to atone for me
Thou didst choose to be tormented
That my doom should be prevented

Hail, Thou Once Despised Jesus, LSB 531, CSB 60, ELH 270

Hail, O once-despised Jesus
Hail, O Galilean King
You have suffered to release us
hope to give and peace to bring
Hail, O universal Savior
bearer of our sin and shame
by your merits we find favor
life is given through your name

Paschal Lamb, by God appointed
all our sins were on you were laid
by almighty love anointed
you have full atonement made
Ev'ry sin has been forgiven
through the power of your blood
open is the gate of heave
we are reconciled to God

The Lamb, LSB 547

The Lamb, the Lamb
As wayward sheep their shepherd kill
So still, His will
On our behalf the Law to fill

He signs, He dies
He takes my sin and wretchedness

He lives, forgives
He give me His own righteousness

I Lay My Sins on Jesus, LSB 606

I lay my sins on Jesus
the spotless Lamb of God
he bears them all, and frees us
from the accursed load
I bring my guilt to Jesus
to wash my crimson stains
white in his blood most precious
till not a spot remains

O Lord, We Praise Thee, LSB 617, ELH 327

May Thy body, Lord, born of Mary
That our sins and sorrows did carry
And Thy blood for us plead
In all trial, fear, and need
Lord, Thy kindness did so constrain Thee
That Thy blood should bless and sustain me
All our debt Thou has paid
Peace with God once more is made

Salvation unto Us Has Come, LSB 555, AH 410, CW1993 390, CW2021 558, ELH 227

Yet as the Law must be fulfilled
Or we must die despairing
Christ came and hath God's anger stilled
Our human nature sharing
He hath for us the Law obeyed
And thus the Father's vengeance stayed
Which over us impended

Since Christ hath full atonement made
And brought to us salvation
Each Christian therefore may be glad
And build on this foundation
Thy grace alone, dear Lord, I plead
Thy death is now my life indeed

For Thou hast paid my ransom

Thy Works, Not Mine, O Christ, LSB 565, CSB 68

Thy works, not mine, O Christ
Speak gladness to this heart
They tell me all is done
They bid my fear depart

Refrain: To whom save Thee, Who canst alone,
For sin atone, Lord, shall I flee

Thy wounds, not mine, O Christ
Can heal my bruised soul
Thy stripes, not mine, contain
The balm that makes me whole

To whom save Thee, who canst alone
For sin atone, Lord, shall I flee
Thy cross, not mine, O Christ
Has borne the awe-full load

Of sins that none could bear
But the incarnate God
To whom save Thee, who canst alone
For sin atone, Lord, shall I flee

Thy death, not mine, O Christ
Has paid the ransom due
Ten thousand deaths like mine
Would have been all too few

To whom save Thee, who canst alone
For sin atone, Lord, shall I flee
Thy righteousness, O Christ
Alone can cover me

No righteousness avails
Save that which is of Thee
To whom save Thee, who canst alone

For sin atone, Lord, shall I flee

If Your Beloved Son, O God, LSB 568

If Thy beloved Son, O God
Had not to earth descended
And in our mortal flesh and blood
Had not sin's power ended
Then this poor, wretched soul of mine
In hell eternally would pine
Because of its transgression

But now I find sweet peace and rest
Despair no more reigns o'er me
No more am I by sin oppressed
For Christ has borne sin for me
Upon the cross for me He died
That, reconciled, I might abide
With Thee, my God, forever.

I trust in Him with all my heart
Now all my sorrow ceases
His words abiding peace impart
His blood from guilt releases
Free grace through Him I now obtain
He washes me from ev'ry stain
And pure I stand before Him

Saved through my Savior's precious blood
I am rejoicing ever
Naught from Thy grace, O Lord, my God
My ransomed soul can sever
All that my blest Redeemer's death
Hath won for me, is mine through faith
And Satan cannot harm me

All righteousness by works is vain
The Law brings condemnation
True righteousness by faith I gain
Christ's work is my salvation

His death, that perfect sacrifice
Has paid the all-sufficient price
In Him my hope is anchored

My guilt, O Father, Thou hast laid
On Christ, Thy Son, my Savior
Lord Jesus, Thou my debt hast paid
And gained for me God's favor
O Holy Ghost, Thou Fount of grace
The good in me to Thee I trace
In faith do Thou preserve me.

Before the Throne of God Above, LSB 574, CW2021 561

Because the sinless Savior died
My sinful soul is counted free
For God, the Just, is satisfied
To look on Him and pardon me

Behold Him there, the risen Lamb
My perfect, spotless Righteousness
The great unchangeable I AM
The King of glory and of grace

One with Himself, I cannot die
My soul is purchased by His blood
My life is hid with Christ on high
With Christ, my Savior and my God

The Gospel Shows the Father's Grace, LSB 580

The Gospel shows the Father's grace
Who sent His Son to save our race
Proclaims how Jesus lived and died
That man might thus be justified

It sets the Lamb before our eyes
Who made the atoning sacrifice
And calls the souls with guilt opprest
To come and find eternal rest

It brings the Savior's righteousness
Our souls to robe in royal dress
From all our guilt it brings release
And gives the troubled conscience peace

What Is This Bread, LSB 629

What is this bread
Christ's body risen from the dead
This bread we break
This life we take
Was crushed to pay for our release
O taste and see the Lord is peace

What is this wine
The blood of Jesus shed for mine
The cup of grace
Brings His embrace
Of life and love until I sing
O taste and see the Lord is King

So who am I
That I should live and He should die
Under the rod
My God, my God
Why have You not forsaken me
O taste and see the Lord is free

Christ, the life of all the living, SBH 79, CSB 98

Thou, O Christ, hast taken on thee
Bitter strokes, a cruel rod
Pain and scorn were heaped upon thee
O thou sinless Son of God
Only thus for me to win
Rescue from the bonds of sin

Thou didst bear the smiting only
That it might not fall on me
Stoodest falsely charged and lonely
That I might be safe and free

Comfortless that I might know
Comfort from thy boundless woe

Your Heart, O God, Is Grieved, LSB 945

Your heart, O God, is grieved we know
By ev'ry evil, ev'ry woe
Upon Your cross forsaken Son
Our death is laid and peace is won

Your arms extend, O Christ, to save
From sting of death and grasp of grave
Your scars before the Father move
His heart to mercy at such love

Glory to God, We Give You Thanks and Praise
Lord Jesus Christ, the Father's only Son
You bore for us the load of this world's sin
O Lamb of God, Your glorious victory won

There is a green hill far away, SBH 77, AH 67

There is a green hill far away
Without a city wall
Where the dear Lord was crucified
Who died to save us all

We may not know, we cannot tell
What pains He had to bear
But we believe it was for us
He hung and suffered there

He died that we might be forgiven,
He died to make us good
That we might go at last to heaven
Saved by His precious blood

There was no other good enough
To pay the price of sin,
He only could unlock the gate
Of heaven, and let us in

Oh, dearly, dearly has He loved
And died our sins to bear
We trust in His redeeming blood
And life eternal share

Ah, holy Jesus, how has thou offended, SBH 85, CSB 99

Lo, the good Shepherd for the sheep is offered
The slave hath sinned, and the Son hath suffered
For man's atonement, while he nothing heedeth
God intercedeth

For me, kind Jesus, was thine Incarnation
Thy mortal sorrow, and the life's oblation
Thy death of anguish and thy bitter Passion
For my salvation

Deep were his wounds, and red, SBH 80

Deep were his wounds, and red
On cruel Calvary
As on the Cross he bled
In bitter agony
But they, whom sin has wounded sore
Find healing in the wounds he bore

He suffered shame and scorn
And wretched, dire disgrace
Forsaken and forlorn
He hung there in our place
But such as would from sin be free
Look to his Cross for victory

His life, his all, he gave
When he was crucified
Our burdened souls to save
What fearful death he died
But each of us, though dead to sin
Through him eternal life may win

O World, See Here Suspended, AH 79

O world, see here suspended
His loving arms extended
Thy Savior on the cross
The Prince of life is willing
All righteousness fulfilling
To suffer anguish, scorn, and loss

O Thou, who hearts dost quicken
Why art Thou sorrow stricken
Why all this nameless pain
While we must make confession
Of sin and dire transgression
No sin on Thee hath left a stain

'Tis I who sins encumber
Whose misdeeds far outnumber
The sands upon the shore
I caused Thy condemnation
Thy deep humiliation
And all the wounds that pain Thee sore

Death for a time must hold Thee
The grave too must enfold Thee
Lest I should be its prey
Death, who for me had tarried
Death now himself lies buried
And I shall live with Thee for aye

There Is A Fountain Filled with Blood, CSB 77, TLH 157, ELH 301

There is a fountain filled with blood
Drawn from Immanuel's vein
And sinners, plunged beneath that flood
Lose all their guilty stains
The dying thief rejoiced to see
That fountain in his day
And there may I, though vile as he
Wash all my sins away

Dear dying Lamb, Thy precious blood
Shall never lose its power
Till all the ransomed Church of God
Be saved, to sin no more:
E'er since by faith I saw the stream
Thy flowing wounds supply
Redeeming love has been my theme
And shall be till I die

Jesus, Savior, Son of God, CSB 78

Jesus, Savior, Son of God
Bearer of the sinner's load
Breaker of the captive's chains
Cleanser of the guilty's stains

Thou the sinner's death hath died
Thou for us wast crucified
For our sins They flesh was torn
Thou our penalty has borne

Savior, Surety, Lamb of God
Thou hast bought us with Thy Blood
Thou hast wiped the debt away
Nothing left for us to pay

Nothing left for us to bear
Nothing left for us to share
But the pardon and the bliss
But the love, the light, the peace

Lord Jesus, Thou Art Going Forth, TLH 150

(The Soul) Lord Jesus, Thou art going forth
For me Thy life to offer
For me, a sinner from my birth
Who cause all Thou must suffer
So be it, then, Thou Hope of men
The I shall follow weeping
Tears flowing free Thy pain to see
Watch o'er Thy sorrows keeping

(Jesus) O Soul, attend though and behold
The fruit of they transgression
My portion is the curse of old
And for man's sin My Passion
Now comes the nigh of sin's dread might
Man's guilt I here am bearing
Oh, weight it, Soul; I make thee whole
No need now of despairing

(The Soul) 'Tis I, Lord Jesus, I confess
Who should have borne sin's wages
And lost the peace of heavenly bliss
Through everlasting ages
Instead 'tis Thou Who goest now
My punishment to carry
The death and blood Lead me to God
By grace I there may tarry

(Jesus) O Soul, I take upon Me now
The pain thou shouldest have suffered
Behold, with grace I thee endow
Grace freely to the offered
The curse I choose that thou mightiest lose
Sin's curse and guilt forever
My fit of love from heaven above
Will give the blessing ever

O Sinner, Come Thy Sin to Mourn, ELH 272

O sinner, come thy sin to mourn
So vast and vile that it has borne
Christ to this vale of anguish
Son of a Virgin, sweet and mild
In poverty the Holy Child
Thy Substitute did languish

Behold with faith God's only Son
Come sigh and see what Love has done
To save thee from damnation

The Father cast on Him thy guilt
For thee His precious blood was spilt
To bless thee with salvation

O meditate how painfully
The Lamb of God on Calvary
Has dies for thy transgressions
How dreary was that awful night
Of agony how great the fight
Of His most wondrous Passion

O Son of God, eternal Word
Divine Redeemer, dearest Lord
We marvel at Thy suff'ring
For Thy disgrace, and pain, and shame
We'll ever magnify Thy name
And praise Thy glorious off'ring

The Day Is Surely Drawing Near, LSB 508

O Jesus, who my debt didst pay
And for my sin wast smitten
Within the Book of Life, oh, may
My name be also written
I will not doubt; I trust in Thee
From Satan Thou hast made me free
And from all condemnation

Therefore my Intercessor be
And for Thy blood and merit
Read from Thy book that I am free
With all who life inherit
That I may see Thee face to face
With all Thy saints in that blest place
Which Thou for us hast purchased

Alas! And Did My Savior Bleed, LSB 427, CSB 101, TLH 154, ELH 282

Thy body slain, sweet Jesus, Thine
And bathed in its own blood
While all exposed to wrath divine

The glorious Suff'rer stood

Was it for crimes that I had done
He groaned upon the tree
Amazing pity, grace unknown
And love beyond degree

Well might the sun in darkness hid
And shut his glories in
When God, the mighty maker died
For His own creatures' sin

When O'er My Sins I Sorrow, TLH 152, ELH 276

When o'er my sin I sorrow
Lord I will look to Thee
And hence my comfort borrow
That Thou wast slain for me
Yea, Lord, Thy precious blood was split
For me, O most unworthy
To take away my guilt

My manifold transgression
Henceforth can harm me none
Since Jesus' bloody Passion
From me God's grace hath won
His precious blood my debts hath paid
Of hell all its torments I am no more afraid

All My Heart Again Rejoices, LSB 360

Should we fear our God's displeasure
Who, to save
Freely gave
His most precious treasure
To redeem us He has given
His own Son
Now is one
Without our blood forever

See the Lamb, our sin once taking

To the cross
Suff'ring loss
Full atonement making
For our life His own He tenders
And His grace
All our race
Fit for glory renders

Not All the Blood of Beasts, LSB 431, TLH 155, ELH 305, CW1993 128, CW2021 398, LW 99

Not all the blood of beasts
On Jewish altars slain
Could give the guilty conscience peace
Or wash away the stain

But Christ, the heavenly Lamb
Takes all our sins away
A sacrifice of nobler name
And richer blood than they

My faith would lay its hand
On that dear head of Thine
While as a penitent I stand
And there confess my sin

My soul looks back to see
The burden Thou didst bear
When hanging on the cursed tree
I know my guilt was there

Believing, we rejoice
To see the curse remove
We bless the Lamb with cheerful voice
And sing His bleeding love

Jesus, Greatest at the Table, LSB 446

Jesus took the role of servant
when upon that gruesome span
for all human sin he suffered

as a vile and loathsome man
on the cross poured out like water
to fulfill the Father's plan.

Can we fathom such deep mercy
Do we see what God has done
Who can grasp this great reversal
love that gives his only Son
Christ, the sinless for the sinners
for the many dies the One

Jesus, Thy Blood and Righteousness, LSB 563

Jesus, Thy blood and righteousness
My beauty are, my glorious dress
Midst flaming worlds, in these arrayed
With joy shall I lift up my head

Bold shall I stand in that great day
Cleansed and redeemed, no debt to pay
Fully absolved through these I am
From sin and fear, from guilt and shame

Lord, I believe Thy precious blood
Which at the mercy seat of God
Pleas for the captives' liberty
Was also shed in love for me

Lord, I believe, were sinners more
Than sands upon the ocean shore
Thou hast for all a ransom paid
For all a full atonement made

When from the dust of death I rise
To claim my mansion in the skies
This then shall be my only plea
Jesus hath lived and died for me

Jesus, be endless praise to Thee
Whose boundless mercy hath for me

For me, and all Thy hands have made
An everlasting ransom paid

Christ Sits at God's Right Hand, LSB 564

Christ's altar was the tree
Where on the world's behalf
Who shed a blood unlike the blood
Of goat or calf
To seal God's guarantee
Of grace that cannot fail
With blood He entered for our good
Behind the veil

What costly sacrifice
To cover human sin
Who but Christ Jesus had the right
To enter in
His blood, that sprinkled price
So we might be assured
That our inheritance in light
Has been secured

Implicit

This category includes expressions of vicarious satisfaction that are implicit. Coming to the texts with a knowledge of Scripture, catechization in home and congregation, and familiarity with the confessions of the *Book of Concord*, one easily sees vicarious satisfaction in them. But as evidence, they hold a lower rank because of arguments the adversaries might make.

In Silent Pain the Eternal Son, LSB 432

In silent pain the eternal Son
Hangs derelict and still
In darkened day His work is done
Fulfilled His Father's will
Uplifted for the world to see
He hangs in strangest victory
For in His body on the tree

He carries all our ill

For peace He came and met its cost
He gave Himself to save the lost
He loved us to the uttermost
And paid for our release

> These lyrics are categorized as implicitly rather than expressly confessing vicarious satisfaction because: the term "our ill" likely embraces the guilt of sin, but the adversaries might argue that it only contemplates the consequences of sin; "met its cost" has an unclear antecedent reference either to peace or our ill; "save the lost" in and of itself could speak to Christus Victor, ransom, covering, or other themes of the atonement without embracing vicarious satisfaction; "paid for our release" could be pure ransom language. Companion to the Hymns sees vicarious satisfaction in this stanza.[37]

Jesus, I Will Ponder Now, LSB 440, ELH 287

Yet, O Lord, not thus alone
Make me see Thy Passion
But its cause to me make known
And its termination.
Ah! I also and my sin
Wrought Thy deep affliction
This indeed the cause hath been
Of Thy crucifixion

> This stanza is included as confessing vicarious satisfaction on the strength of the commentary in *Companion to the Hymns* that it sings "His vicarious death."[38]

---

[37] *Companion to the Hymns*, I:263.

[38] *Companion to the Hymns*, I:285.

No Temple Now, No Gift of Price, LSB 530

> The dying Lord our ransom paid
> One final full self-off'ring made
> Complete in every part
> His finished sacrifice for sins
> The covenant of grace begins

> The adversaries might reject this stanza, but it is included as at least implicitly confessing vicarious satisfaction. It confesses that Christ's self-offering was a sacrifice for sins and a finished sacrifice, with allusions to his cry from the cross and the exposition of his sacrifice in the Epistle to the Hebrews, to say nothing of the rich Levitical background. Furthermore, though Forde claims God could and did just "up and forgive" before and without the coming of Christ or his sacrifice on the cross, the last line explicitly confesses that once Christ finished his self-sacrifice for sins, then "The covenant of grace *begins*." It is a *new* covenant (Jeremiah 31 and Hebrews 8 and 9). In the *Verba*, Christ's Words of Institution of the Lord's Supper, which every Christian knows, the cup of Christ's death and sacrifice is "the *new* covenant *in My blood*, which is *shed* for you." (Luke 22:20, Matthew 26:28, Mark 14;24, 1 Corinthians 11:25, and Hebrews 12:24).

Come, Thou Fount of Every Blessing, LSB 686

> He, to rescue me from danger
> Interposed His precious blood

> The adversaries say that since God all along was ready to "up and forgive" sin, there was no need for anything to interpose. We only needed to believe that God was ready to forgive in a generic mercy and general amnesty. These lyrics confess, however, that Jesus rescued us from danger by interposing his precious blood. The clear implication is that, without the interposition of Christ's blood, there would be no rescue and the danger still would be impending over

us.

We All Believe in One True God, LSB 654

Born of Mary, virgin mother
By the power of the Spirit
Word made flesh, our elder brother
That the lost might life inherit
Was crucified for all our sin
And raised by God to life again

Who the Church, His own creation
Keeps in unity of Spirit
Here forgiveness and salvation
Daily comes through Jesus merit

Bibliography

Anselm. *Cur Deus Homo*. trans. Sidney Norton Deane. Fort Worth: RDMc Publishing, 2005, 1903.

Aubert, Annette G. 2002. "Luther, Melanchthon, and Chemnitz: The Doctrine of the Atonement with Special Reference to Gustaf Aulen's Christus Victor." ThM Thesis. Westminster Theological Seminary.

Aulén, Gustaf, *Christus Victor: An Historical Study of the Three Main Types of the Idea of the Atonement*, trans. A. G. Hebert. New York: Macmillan Publishing Co., Inc., 1969.

Dau, William Herman Theodore. "Did God Have to be Reconciled by the Death of Christ?" *Theological Quarterly*, vol. XX, no. 1, January 1916, pp. 1-13.

David Chytraeus. *Chytraeus on Sacrifice: A Reformation Treatise in biblical Theology*, trans. John Warwick Montgomery. St Louis: Concordia Publishing House, 1962.

Denny, James. *The Death of Christ: Its Place and Interpretation in the New Testament*, 5th ed. New York: A. C. Armstrong, 1907.

Dierks, Theodore. *Reconciliation and Justification*. St. Louis: Concordia Publishing House, 1938.

Eckardt, Burnell F. Jr. *Anselm and Luther on the Atonement: Was it Necessary?* San Francisco: Mellen Research University Press, 1992.

Forde, Gerhard O. "Caught in the Act: Reflections on the Work of Christ," *World in World*, 3/1 1983, 22-31.

Forde, Gerhard O. "In Our Place," in *A More Radical Gospel: Essays on Eschatology, Authority, Atonement, and Ecumenism*, Mark C. Mattes and Steven D. Paulson, eds. (Minneapolis: Fortress Press, 2017), 101-113.

Forde, Gerhard O. *The Law-Gospel Debate*. Minneapolis: Fortress Press, 2007.

Forde, Gerhard O. "The Work of Christ" in Carl E. Braaten and Robert W. Jensen, eds., *Christian Dogmatics*. Philadelphia: Fortress Press, 1984, II 1-99.

Forde, Gerhard O. *Theology Is for Proclamation*. Minneapolis: Fortress Press, 1990.

Franzman, Martin H. "Reconciliation and Justification," *Concordia Theological Monthly*, vol. XXI, no. 2, 1950, pp. 81-93.

Gerhard, Johann. *An Explanation of the History of the Suffering and Death of Our Lord Jesus Christ*, Elmer M. Hohle, trans. Malone, TX: Repristination Press, 1998.

Gerhard, Johann. *On Justification through Faith*, Richard J. Dinda, trans. St. Louis: Concordia Publishing House, 2018, 52-109.

Gibbs, Jeffrey A. "The Son of God and the Father's Wrath: Atonement and Salvation in Matthew's Gospel," *Concordia Theological Quarterly*, vol. 72, no. 3, 2008, pp. 211-225.

Gieschen, Charles A. "Editorial." *Concordia Theological Quarterly*, vol. 72, no. 3, 2008, p. 194.

Gieschen, Charles A. "The Death of Jesus in the Gospel of John: Atonement for Sin?" *Concordia Theological Quarterly*, vol. 72, no. 3, 2008, pp. 243-61.

Grensted, Laurence William. *A Short History of the Doctrine of the Atonement*. London: University of Manchester Press, 1920.

Grensted, Laurence William. *The Atonement in History and Life*. London: Society for Promoting Christian Knowledge, 1929.

Hengel, Martin. *The Atonement: The Origins of the Doctrine in the New Testament*. Minneapolis: Fortress Press, 1981.

Jenson, Robert W. *Systematic Theology: the Triune God*.Oxford: Oxford University Press, 1997, I.165-206.

Judisch, Douglas. "Propitiation in the Language and Typology of the Old Testament," *Concordia Theological Quarterly*, vol. 48, nos. 2 & 3, 1984, pp. 221-243.

Just, Arthur A. Jr. "The Cross, the Atonement, and the Eucharist in Luke." *Concordia Theological Quarterly*, vol. 84, no. 3-4, 2020, pp. 227-244.

Kilcrease, Jack D. "*Heilsgeschicte* and Atonement in the Theology of Johannes Christian Konrad von Hofmann (1810-1877): An Exposition and Critique," *Logia: A Journal of Lutheran Theology* 22, no. 2 (2013).

Kilcrease, Jack D. "Johann Gerhard, the Socinians, and Modern Rejections of Substitutionary Atonement," *Concordia Theological Quarterly*, vol. 83, nos. 1-2, 2018, pp. 19-44.

Kilcrease, Jack D. *The Doctrine of Atonement: From Luther to Forde.* Eugene, OR: Wipf & Stock, 2018.

Kilcrease, Jack D. *The Work of Christ: Revisionist Doctrine and the Confessional Lutheran Response* (Eugene, OR: Wipf & Stock, 2018).

Kleinig, John W. "Sacrificial Atonement by Jesus and God's Wrath in the Light of the Old Testament." *Concordia Theological Quarterly*, vol. 84, no. 3-4, 2020, pp. 195-208.

Long, Thomas E. *The Viability of a Sacrificial Theology of Atonement: A Critique and Analysis of Traditional and Transformational Views.* Minneapolis: Lutheran University Press, 2006.

Luther, Martin. *The 1529 Holy Week and Easter Sermons of Dr. Martin Luther.* Trans Irving L. Sandberg. St. Louis: Concordia Publishing House, 1998.

Maier, Walter A. III. "Penal Substitutionary Atonement?" *Concordia theological Quarterly*, vol. 84, no. 3-4, 2020, pp. 245-263.

Maxfield, John A. "Luther, Zwingli, and Calvin on the Significance of Christ's Death" *Concordia Theological Quarterly*, vol. 75, nos. 1-2, 2011, pp. 91-110.

Masaki, Noamichi. "Contemporary Views on Atonement in Light of the Lutheran Confessions," *Concordia Theological Quarterly*, vol. 72, no. 4, 2008, pp. 305-325.

Morris, Leon, *Glory in the Cross: A Study in Atonement.* Grand Rapids: Baker Book House, 1966.

Morris, Leon. *The Apostolic Preaching of the Cross*, 3rd rev. ed. Grand Rapids: William B. Eerdmans Publishing Company, 1965.

Morris, Leon. *The Atonement: Its Meaning and Significance.* Downers Grove: InterVarsity Press, 1983.

Morris, Leon. *The Cross in the New Testament.* Grand Rapids: William B. Eerdmans Publishing Company, 1965.

Mozley, John Kenneth. *The Doctrine of the Atonement.* New York: Charles Scribner's Sons, 1916.

Pieper, Francis. *Christian Dogmatics*, St. Louis: Concordia Publishing House, 1951, II.330-394

Peters, Albrecht. *Commentary on Luther's Catechisms: Creed*. trans. Thomas Trapp. St. Louis: Concordia Publishing House, 2011.

Preus, Robert D. "The Vicarious Atonement in John Quenstedt," *Concordia Theological Monthly*, vol. xxxii, no. 2, 1961, pp. 78-97.

Quenstedt, Johannes and Robert D. Preus. *Atonement in Lutheran Orthodoxy: Johannes Questedt*. trans. Matthew Carver. Sidney, Montana: Synoptic Text Information Services, Inc., 2023.

Remensnyder, Junius B., *The Atonement and Modern Thought*, Philadelphia: Lutheran Publication Society, 1905.

Scaer, David P. "Flights from the Atonement," *Concordia Theological Quarterly*, vol. 72, no. 3, 2008, pp. 195-210.

Scaer, David P. "The Sacrificial Death of Christ," in *Christology*, (Confessional Lutheran Dogmatics, vol VI). Fort Wayne, IN: The International Foundation for Lutheran Confessional Research, 1989, 66-82.

Scaer, Peter J. "Reckoned Among the Lawless," *Concordia theological Quarterly*, vol. 84, no. 3-4, 2020, pp. 209-225.

Scaer, Peter J. "The Atonement in Mark's Sacramental Theology." *Concordia Theological Quarterly*, vol. 72, no. 3, 2008, pp. 227-242.

Schdmid, Heinrich. *Doctrinal Theology of the Evangelical Lutheran Church*. Minneapolis: Augsburg Publishing House, 1875, 1889, 342-370.

Tanner, Jacob. *Atonement and Forgiveness: A Re-Orientation*. Minneapolis: Augsburg Publishing House, 1948.

Williams, George Hunston. *Anselm: Communion and Atonement*. St. Louis: Concordia Publishing House, 1960.